50% OFF Online Praxis Teaching Reading Elementary Education Prep Course!

Dear Customer,

We consider it an honor and a privilege that you chose our Praxis Teaching Reading Elementary Education Study Guide. As a way of showing our appreciation and to help us better serve you, we have partnered with Mometrix Test Preparation to offer you **50% off their online Praxis Teaching Reading Elementary Education Prep Course**. Many Praxis Teaching Reading Elementary Education courses are needlessly expensive and don't deliver enough value. With their course, you get access to the best Praxis Teaching Reading Elementary Education prep material, and **you only pay half price**.

Mometrix has structured our online course to perfectly complement your printed study guide. The Praxis Teaching Reading Prep Course contains **in-depth lessons** that cover all the most important topics, **20+ video reviews** that explain difficult concepts, over **300 practice questions** to ensure you feel prepared, and **300 digital flashcards**, so you can study while you're on the go.

Online Praxis Teaching Reading Elementary Education Prep Course

Topics Included:
- Phonological and Phonemic Awareness
- Phonics and Decoding
- Vocabulary and Fluency
- Comprehension of Literacy and Informational Texts
- Writing
- Assessment and Instructional Decision Making

Course Features:

Praxis 5205 Study Guide
- Get content that complements our best-selling study guide.

Full-Length Practice Tests
- With over 300 practice questions, you can test yourself again and again.

Mobile Friendly
- If you need to study on the go, the course is easily accessible from your mobile device.

Praxis Teaching Reading Flashcards
- Our course includes a flashcard mode with 300 content cards to help you study.

To receive this discount, visit them at mometrix.com/university/praxis5205 or simply scan this QR code with your smartphone. At the checkout page, enter the discount code: **5205TPB50**

If you have any questions or concerns, please contact them at support@mometrix.com.

 in partnership wit

FREE Test Taking Tips DVD Offer

To help us better serve you, we have developed a Test Taking Tips DVD that we would like to give you for FREE. **This DVD covers world-class test taking tips that you can use to be even more successful when you are taking your test.**

All that we ask is that you email us your feedback about your study guide. Please let us know what you thought about it – whether that is good, bad or indifferent.

To get your **FREE Test Taking Tips DVD**, email freedvd@studyguideteam.com with "FREE DVD" in the subject line and the following information in the body of the email:

    a. The title of your study guide.

    b. Your product rating on a scale of 1-5, with 5 being the highest rating.

    c. Your feedback about the study guide. What did you think of it?

    d. Your full name and shipping address to send your free DVD.

If you have any questions or concerns, please don't hesitate to contact us at freedvd@studyguideteam.com.

Thanks again!

Praxis Teaching Reading Elementary 5205 Study Guide

Exam Prep and Practice Test Questions
[Includes Detailed Answer Explanations]

Joshua Rueda

Copyright © 2023 by TPB Publishing

All rights reserved. No part of this publication may be reproduced, distributed, or transmitted in any form or by any means, including photocopying, recording, or other electronic or mechanical methods, without the prior written permission of the publisher, except in the case of brief quotations embodied in critical reviews and certain other noncommercial uses permitted by copyright law.

Written and edited by TPB Publishing.

TPB Publishing is not associated with or endorsed by any official testing organization. TPB Publishing is a publisher of unofficial educational products. All test and organization names are trademarks of their respective owners. Content in this book is included for utilitarian purposes only and does not constitute an endorsement by TPB Publishing of any particular point of view.

Interested in buying more than 10 copies of our product? Contact us about bulk discounts:
bulkorders@studyguideteam.com

ISBN 13: 9781637752081
ISBN 10: 1637752083

Table of Contents

Welcome ---- 1
   FREE Videos/DVD OFFER ---- 1

Quick Overview ---- 2

Test-Taking Strategies ---- 3

Introduction ---- 7

Study Prep Plan for the Praxis 5205 ---- 11

Phonological & Phonemic Awareness Including Emergent Literacy ---- 13
   Practice Quiz ---- 19
   Answer Explanations ---- 20

Phonics and Decoding ---- 21
   Practice Quiz ---- 31
   Answer Explanations ---- 32

Vocabulary and Fluency ---- 33
   Practice Quiz ---- 42
   Answer Explanations ---- 43

Comprehension of Literary and Informational Text ---- 44
   Practice Quiz ---- 66
   Answer Explanations ---- 67

Writing ---- 68
   Written Expression ---- 68
   Spelling and Grammar ---- 75
   Practice Quiz ---- 81

Assessment and Instructional Decision Making (Constructed Response) --- *82*

Practice Test -- *83*

    Constructed Response 1 --- 96

    Constructed Response 2 --- 96

    Constructed Response 3 --- 97

Answer Explanations --- *98*

Index --- *110*

Welcome

Dear Reader,

Welcome to your new Test Prep Books study guide! We are pleased that you chose us to help you prepare for your exam. There are many study options to choose from, and we appreciate you choosing us. Studying can be a daunting task, but we have designed a smart, effective study guide to help prepare you for what lies ahead.

Whether you're a parent helping your child learn and grow, a high school student working hard to get into your dream college, or a nursing student studying for a complex exam, we want to help give you the tools you need to succeed. We hope this study guide gives you the skills and the confidence to thrive, and we can't thank you enough for allowing us to be part of your journey.

In an effort to continue to improve our products, we welcome feedback from our customers. We look forward to hearing from you. Suggestions, success stories, and criticisms can all be communicated by emailing us at info@studyguideteam.com.

Sincerely,
Test Prep Books Team

FREE Videos/DVD OFFER

Doing well on your exam requires both knowing the test content and understanding how to use that knowledge to do well on the test. We offer completely FREE test taking tip videos. **These videos cover world-class tips that you can use to succeed on your test.**

To get your **FREE videos**, you can use the QR code below or email freevideos@studyguideteam.com with "Free Videos" in the subject line and the following information in the body of the email:

    a. The title of your product
    b. Your product rating on a scale of 1-5, with 5 being the highest
    c. Your feedback about the product

If you have any questions or concerns, please don't hesitate to contact us at info@studyguideteam.com.

Quick Overview

As you draw closer to taking your exam, effective preparation becomes more and more important. Thankfully, you have this study guide to help you get ready. Use this guide to help keep your studying on track and refer to it often.

This study guide contains several key sections that will help you be successful on your exam. The guide contains tips for what you should do the night before and the day of the test. Also included are test-taking tips. Knowing the right information is not always enough. Many well-prepared test takers struggle with exams. These tips will help equip you to accurately read, assess, and answer test questions.

A large part of the guide is devoted to showing you what content to expect on the exam and to helping you better understand that content. In this guide are practice test questions so that you can see how well you have grasped the content. Then, answer explanations are provided so that you can understand why you missed certain questions.

Don't try to cram the night before you take your exam. This is not a wise strategy for a few reasons. First, your retention of the information will be low. Your time would be better used by reviewing information you already know rather than trying to learn a lot of new information. Second, you will likely become stressed as you try to gain a large amount of knowledge in a short amount of time. Third, you will be depriving yourself of sleep. So be sure to go to bed at a reasonable time the night before. Being well-rested helps you focus and remain calm.

Be sure to eat a substantial breakfast the morning of the exam. If you are taking the exam in the afternoon, be sure to have a good lunch as well. Being hungry is distracting and can make it difficult to focus. You have hopefully spent lots of time preparing for the exam. Don't let an empty stomach get in the way of success!

When travelling to the testing center, leave earlier than needed. That way, you have a buffer in case you experience any delays. This will help you remain calm and will keep you from missing your appointment time at the testing center.

Be sure to pace yourself during the exam. Don't try to rush through the exam. There is no need to risk performing poorly on the exam just so you can leave the testing center early. Allow yourself to use all of the allotted time if needed.

Remain positive while taking the exam even if you feel like you are performing poorly. Thinking about the content you should have mastered will not help you perform better on the exam.

Once the exam is complete, take some time to relax. Even if you feel that you need to take the exam again, you will be well served by some down time before you begin studying again. It's often easier to convince yourself to study if you know that it will come with a reward!

Test-Taking Strategies

1. Predicting the Answer

When you feel confident in your preparation for a multiple-choice test, try predicting the answer before reading the answer choices. This is especially useful on questions that test objective factual knowledge. By predicting the answer before reading the available choices, you eliminate the possibility that you will be distracted or led astray by an incorrect answer choice. You will feel more confident in your selection if you read the question, predict the answer, and then find your prediction among the answer choices. After using this strategy, be sure to still read all of the answer choices carefully and completely. If you feel unprepared, you should not attempt to predict the answers. This would be a waste of time and an opportunity for your mind to wander in the wrong direction.

2. Reading the Whole Question

Too often, test takers scan a multiple-choice question, recognize a few familiar words, and immediately jump to the answer choices. Test authors are aware of this common impatience, and they will sometimes prey upon it. For instance, a test author might subtly turn the question into a negative, or he or she might redirect the focus of the question right at the end. The only way to avoid falling into these traps is to read the entirety of the question carefully before reading the answer choices.

3. Looking for Wrong Answers

Long and complicated multiple-choice questions can be intimidating. One way to simplify a difficult multiple-choice question is to eliminate all of the answer choices that are clearly wrong. In most sets of answers, there will be at least one selection that can be dismissed right away. If the test is administered on paper, the test taker could draw a line through it to indicate that it may be ignored; otherwise, the test taker will have to perform this operation mentally or on scratch paper. In either case, once the obviously incorrect answers have been eliminated, the remaining choices may be considered.

Sometimes identifying the clearly wrong answers will give the test taker some information about the correct answer. For instance, if one of the remaining answer choices is a direct opposite of one of the eliminated answer choices, it may well be the correct answer. The opposite of obviously wrong is obviously right! Of course, this is not always the case. Some answers are obviously incorrect simply because they are irrelevant to the question being asked. Still, identifying and eliminating some incorrect answer choices is a good way to simplify a multiple-choice question.

4. Don't Overanalyze

Anxious test takers often overanalyze questions. When you are nervous, your brain will often run wild, causing you to make associations and discover clues that don't actually exist. If you feel that this may be a problem for you, do whatever you can to slow down during the test. Try taking a deep breath or counting to ten. As you read and consider the question, restrict yourself to the particular words used by the author. Avoid thought tangents about what the author *really* meant, or what he or she was *trying* to say. The only things that matter on a multiple-choice test are the words that are actually in the question. You must avoid reading too much into a multiple-choice question, or supposing that the writer meant something other than what he or she wrote.

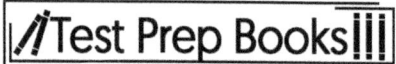

Test-Taking Strategies

5. No Need for Panic

It is wise to learn as many strategies as possible before taking a multiple-choice test, but it is likely that you will come across a few questions for which you simply don't know the answer. In this situation, avoid panicking. Because most multiple-choice tests include dozens of questions, the relative value of a single wrong answer is small. As much as possible, you should compartmentalize each question on a multiple-choice test. In other words, you should not allow your feelings about one question to affect your success on the others. When you find a question that you either don't understand or don't know how to answer, just take a deep breath and do your best. Read the entire question slowly and carefully. Try rephrasing the question a couple of different ways. Then, read all of the answer choices carefully. After eliminating obviously wrong answers, make a selection and move on to the next question.

6. Confusing Answer Choices

When working on a difficult multiple-choice question, there may be a tendency to focus on the answer choices that are the easiest to understand. Many people, whether consciously or not, gravitate to the answer choices that require the least concentration, knowledge, and memory. This is a mistake. When you come across an answer choice that is confusing, you should give it extra attention. A question might be confusing because you do not know the subject matter to which it refers. If this is the case, don't eliminate the answer before you have affirmatively settled on another. When you come across an answer choice of this type, set it aside as you look at the remaining choices. If you can confidently assert that one of the other choices is correct, you can leave the confusing answer aside. Otherwise, you will need to take a moment to try to better understand the confusing answer choice. Rephrasing is one way to tease out the sense of a confusing answer choice.

7. Your First Instinct

Many people struggle with multiple-choice tests because they overthink the questions. If you have studied sufficiently for the test, you should be prepared to trust your first instinct once you have carefully and completely read the question and all of the answer choices. There is a great deal of research suggesting that the mind can come to the correct conclusion very quickly once it has obtained all of the relevant information. At times, it may seem to you as if your intuition is working faster even than your reasoning mind. This may in fact be true. The knowledge you obtain while studying may be retrieved from your subconscious before you have a chance to work out the associations that support it. Verify your instinct by working out the reasons that it should be trusted.

8. Key Words

Many test takers struggle with multiple-choice questions because they have poor reading comprehension skills. Quickly reading and understanding a multiple-choice question requires a mixture of skill and experience. To help with this, try jotting down a few key words and phrases on a piece of scrap paper. Doing this concentrates the process of reading and forces the mind to weigh the relative importance of the question's parts. In selecting words and phrases to write down, the test taker thinks about the question more deeply and carefully. This is especially true for multiple-choice questions that are preceded by a long prompt.

9. Subtle Negatives

One of the oldest tricks in the multiple-choice test writer's book is to subtly reverse the meaning of a question with a word like *not* or *except*. If you are not paying attention to each word in the question, you can easily be led astray by this trick. For instance, a common question format is, "Which of the following is...?" Obviously, if the question instead is, "Which of the following is not...?," then the answer will be quite different. Even worse, the test makers are aware of the potential for this mistake and will include one answer choice that would be correct if the question were not negated or reversed. A test taker who misses the reversal will find what he or she believes to be a correct answer and will be so confident that he or she will fail to reread the question and discover the original error. The only way to avoid this is to practice a wide variety of multiple-choice questions and to pay close attention to each and every word.

10. Reading Every Answer Choice

It may seem obvious, but you should always read every one of the answer choices! Too many test takers fall into the habit of scanning the question and assuming that they understand the question because they recognize a few key words. From there, they pick the first answer choice that answers the question they believe they have read. Test takers who read all of the answer choices might discover that one of the latter answer choices is actually *more* correct. Moreover, reading all of the answer choices can remind you of facts related to the question that can help you arrive at the correct answer. Sometimes, a misstatement or incorrect detail in one of the latter answer choices will trigger your memory of the subject and will enable you to find the right answer. Failing to read all of the answer choices is like not reading all of the items on a restaurant menu: you might miss out on the perfect choice.

11. Spot the Hedges

One of the keys to success on multiple-choice tests is paying close attention to every word. This is never truer than with words like almost, most, some, and sometimes. These words are called "hedges" because they indicate that a statement is not totally true or not true in every place and time. An absolute statement will contain no hedges, but in many subjects, the answers are not always straightforward or absolute.

There are always exceptions to the rules in these subjects. For this reason, you should favor those multiple-choice questions that contain hedging language. The presence of qualifying words indicates that the author is taking special care with their words, which is certainly important when composing the right answer. After all, there are many ways to be wrong, but there is only one way to be right! For this reason, it is wise to avoid answers that are absolute when taking a multiple-choice test. An absolute answer is one that says things are either all one way or all another. They often include words like *every*, *always*, *best*, and *never*. If you are taking a multiple-choice test in a subject that doesn't lend itself to absolute answers, be on your guard if you see any of these words.

12. Long Answers

In many subject areas, the answers are not simple. As already mentioned, the right answer often requires hedges. Another common feature of the answers to a complex or subjective question are qualifying clauses, which are groups of words that subtly modify the meaning of the sentence. If the question or answer choice describes a rule to which there are exceptions or the subject matter is complicated, ambiguous, or confusing, the correct answer will require many words in order to be

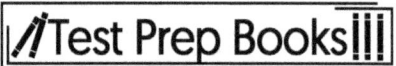

expressed clearly and accurately. In essence, you should not be deterred by answer choices that seem excessively long. Oftentimes, the author of the text will not be able to write the correct answer without offering some qualifications and modifications. Your job is to read the answer choices thoroughly and completely and to select the one that most accurately and precisely answers the question.

13. Restating to Understand

Sometimes, a question on a multiple-choice test is difficult not because of what it asks but because of how it is written. If this is the case, restate the question or answer choice in different words. This process serves a couple of important purposes. First, it forces you to concentrate on the core of the question. In order to rephrase the question accurately, you have to understand it well. Rephrasing the question will concentrate your mind on the key words and ideas. Second, it will present the information to your mind in a fresh way. This process may trigger your memory and render some useful scrap of information picked up while studying.

14. True Statements

Sometimes an answer choice will be true in itself, but it does not answer the question. This is one of the main reasons why it is essential to read the question carefully and completely before proceeding to the answer choices. Too often, test takers skip ahead to the answer choices and look for true statements. Having found one of these, they are content to select it without reference to the question above. Obviously, this provides an easy way for test makers to play tricks. The savvy test taker will always read the entire question before turning to the answer choices. Then, having settled on a correct answer choice, he or she will refer to the original question and ensure that the selected answer is relevant. The mistake of choosing a correct-but-irrelevant answer choice is especially common on questions related to specific pieces of objective knowledge. A prepared test taker will have a wealth of factual knowledge at their disposal, and should not be careless in its application.

15. No Patterns

One of the more dangerous ideas that circulates about multiple-choice tests is that the correct answers tend to fall into patterns. These erroneous ideas range from a belief that B and C are the most common right answers, to the idea that an unprepared test-taker should answer "A-B-A-C-A-D-A-B-A." It cannot be emphasized enough that pattern-seeking of this type is exactly the WRONG way to approach a multiple-choice test.

To begin with, it is highly unlikely that the test maker will plot the correct answers according to some predetermined pattern. The questions are scrambled and delivered in a random order. Furthermore, even if the test maker was following a pattern in the assignation of correct answers, there is no reason why the test taker would know which pattern he or she was using. Any attempt to discern a pattern in the answer choices is a waste of time and a distraction from the real work of taking the test. A test taker would be much better served by extra preparation before the test than by reliance on a pattern in the answers.

Introduction

Function of the Test

The Praxis Teaching Reading: Elementary Education Exam is for students or professionals entering or completing teacher preparation programs. It is required in 40 states for teacher licensure, and scores are transferrable for those wishing to move between states. This exam measures the ability of an individual to teach oral language and reading development at an elementary level. As identified by the National Reading Panel, it covers the five most important aspects of teaching reading instruction: phonemic awareness, phonics, fluency, vocabulary, and comprehension. This exam is offered nationwide through a variety of testing locations. The number of people who took the Praxis Teaching Reading Exam in the 2017–2018 year was 5,079.

Test Administration

The Praxis Teaching Reading Exam is available for test takers each day of each month, whether testing in-person or remote, as of 2022 . You can register to take the exam on the ETS Praxis website, and an available listing of test sites will be available for you to choose from. Retesting is available once every 28 days, or after 28 days for subject tests. Praxis tests are offered through the Educational Testing Service (ETS), and ETS is dedicated to providing accommodations to persons who have disabilities. Some accommodations should be requested, so visit the ETS website to find out more.

Test Format

The testing room prohibits cell phone use, and you are not allowed to bring in personal items, beverages, study materials, pencils, pens, calculators, or any electronic device of any kind. Personal items are not allowed in the test room, so if your facility does not provide storage, you must plan accordingly.

The Praxis Teaching Reading Exam is a 150 minute test with 90 selected-response questions and 3 constructed-response questions.

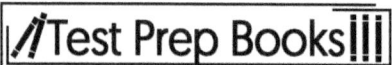

The table below shows a breakdown of the content domains:

Content Category	Number of Questions	Percentage of Exam
• Phonological and Phonemic Awareness Including Emergent Literacy	13	11%
• Phonics and Decoding	18	15%
• Vocabulary and Fluency	21	18%
• Comprehension of Literary and Informational Text	22	18%
• Writing	15	13%
• Assessment and Instructional Decision Making (Constructed Response)	3	25%

Scoring

The passing score for the Praxis Teaching Reading Exam depends on particular state requirements. You will be notified of a passing score after you take the exam and your states have been entered into the system. A list of states and passing scores are also available on the ETS website. The highest score of any other Praxis tests you have taken in the past ten years will show up on your score report along with your new score. End scores reveal how you did in each content, so if you choose to retake the exam, you will know which areas to focus on the most. All scores for Praxis exams are valid for ten years.

Recent/Future Developments

Praxis exams are updated on a regular basis to align with new core content. Test scores, however, will be valid for a ten-year period regardless of whether or not the content is still relevant.

As you study for your test, we'd like to take the opportunity to remind you that you are capable of great things! With the right tools and dedication, you truly can do anything you set your mind to. The fact that you are holding this book right now shows how committed you are. In case no one has told you lately, you've got this! Our intention behind including this coloring page is to give you the chance to take some time to engage your creative side when you need a little brain-break from studying. As a company, we want to encourage people like you to achieve their dreams by providing good quality study materials for the tests and certifications that improve careers and change lives. As individuals, many of us have taken such tests in our careers, and we know how challenging this process can be. While we can't come alongside you and cheer you on personally, we can offer you the space to recall your purpose, reconnect with your passion, and refresh your brain through an artistic practice. We wish you every success, and happy studying!

Study Prep Plan for the Praxis 5205

1 **Schedule** - Use one of our study schedules below or come up with one of your own.

2 **Relax** - Test anxiety can hurt even the best students. There are many ways to reduce stress. Find the one that works best for you.

3 **Execute** - Once you have a good plan in place, be sure to stick to it.

One Week Study Schedule

Day 1	Phonological and Phonemic Awareness...
Day 2	Phonics and Decoding
Day 3	Vocabulary and Fluency
Day 4	Comprehension of Literary...
Day 5	Writing
Day 6	Practice Test
Day 7	Take Your Exam!

Two Week Study Schedule

Day 1	Phonological and Phonemic Awareness...	Day 8	Practice Questions
Day 2	Phonics and Decoding	Day 9	Writing
Day 3	Vocabulary and Fluency	Day 10	Spelling and Grammar
Day 4	Comprehension of Literary and...	Day 11	Practice Questions
Day 5	Differentiate for Appropriate and...	Day 12	Practice Test
Day 6	Literary Devices	Day 13	Answer Explanations
Day 7	Using Technology to Support Students	Day 14	Take Your Exam!

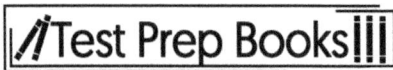

Study Prep Plan for the Praxis 5205

One Month Study Schedule

Day 1	Phonological and Phonemic...	Day 11	Methods of Supporting Fluent Reading...	Day 21	Practice Questions
Day 2	Instructional Methods to Teach Beginning...	Day 12	Practice Questions	Day 22	Writing
Day 3	Practice Questions	Day 13	Comprehension of Literary and...	Day 23	High-Quality Writing
Day 4	Phonics and Decoding	Day 14	Metacognition Guides Students...	Day 24	Digital Tools
Day 5	Blends	Day 15	Differentiate for...	Day 25	Spelling and Grammar
Day 6	Multisensory Approaches for...	Day 16	Genres, Structures, and Features of Literary...	Day 26	Practice Questions
Day 7	Practice Questions	Day 17	Literary Devices	Day 27	Assessment and...
Day 8	Vocabulary and Fluency	Day 18	Types, Structures, and Features of...	Day 28	Practice Test
Day 9	Teaching Word Solving	Day 19	Using Technology to Support Students	Day 29	Answer Explanations
Day 10	Guide Students to Understand...	Day 20	Support Active Learning Across Content Areas	Day 30	Take Your Exam!

Build your own prep plan by visiting:
testprepbooks.com/prep

Phonological & Phonemic Awareness Including Emergent Literacy

Instructional Methods for Teaching Phonological Awareness

Phonological awareness is the conscious realization that words have multiple sounds working together. These word sounds may be distinguishable by syllables, onsets and rimes, or by phonemes (each of which will be covered in this section.) Phonological awareness is critical for the reading and writing processes because written words and spoken words go hand in hand. In order for a reader to move from written word to spoken word, they must be able to recognize the sounds represented in the different parts of a word. In this section, read about the different methods for teaching phonological awareness to new readers.

Recognition of Rhyme and Alliteration
Teaching a child to recognize **rhymes** within words is one of the basic levels of phonological awareness. A child must closely pay attention to the word's different sounds. By teaching them to pay attention to the individual sounds, children also learn that words can be made up of multiple, different parts. They should listen to the sounds within different words and determine if they are similar, meaning they have rhyme, or if they are different, meaning they do not have rhyme.

Teaching a child to recognize **alliteration** in words is similar to that of teaching them to recognize rhyme. Not only is it another early, basic level of phonological awareness, but it also deals with have the child recognize patterns within the sounds of words. **Alliteration** is the consecutive repetition of sound(s) at the beginning of words. Having children listen to the individual word sounds, again, reinforces the idea words are broken up into multiple parts.

Segmenting
When a child recognizes that there are multiple parts of a word and that the word can be broken down into its different sounds, they naturally begin **segmenting** the phonemes in the word. Segmenting is just the child's ability to break the word or words into their individual, specific sounds. For example, a child might break the word "cat" into its individual sounds: /k/ /a/ /t/.

Blending
Blending is essentially the inversion of segmenting. Rather than being presented with the whole word, the child is first presented with the individual sounds of a word and is then asked to "blend" them together to make the intended word. For example, a student might be given the sounds: /k/ /a/ /t/. If the child were to put these sounds together, they would form the word "cat".

Manipulation of Syllables
As students develop their phonological awareness, they may begin manipulating the syllables within words. The **manipulation of syllables** refers to a child "playing" with word sounds to create new words. For example, a student may be given the word "cat" and asked to change the /c/ to a /b/ in order to create a new word. The students would respond that the new word is "bat".

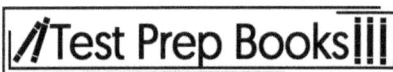

Phonological & Phonemic Awareness Including Emergent Literacy

<u>Onset and Rime</u>

Onset refers to the consonants that occur before a vowel. It is the initial phonological piece of any word. **Rime** refers to the letters that follow after the onset. For example, in the word "cat," the "c" would be the onset, and "at" would be the rime.

Instructional Methods for Teaching Phonemic Awareness

Phonemic Awareness in Reading Development

A **phoneme** is the smallest unit of sound in a given language and is one aspect under the umbrella of skills associated with phonological awareness. A child demonstrates phonemic awareness when identifying rhymes, recognizing alliterations, and isolating specific sounds inside a word or a set of words. Students who demonstrate basic **phonemic awareness** will eventually also be able to blend together a variety of phonemes independently and appropriately.

Some classroom strategies to strengthen phonemic awareness may include:

- Introduction to nursery rhymes and word play
- Introduces speech discrimination techniques to train the ear to hear more accurately
- Repeated instruction connecting sounds to letters and blending sounds
- Use of visual images coupled with corresponding sounds and words
- Teaching speech sounds through direct instruction
- Comparing known to unfamiliar words
- Practicing pronunciation of newly introduced letters, letter combinations, and words
- Practicing word decoding
- Differentiating similar sounding words

Development of Phonemic-Awareness Skills

Age-appropriate and developmentally appropriate instruction for phonological and phonemic awareness is key to helping children strengthen their reading and writing skills. Phonological and phonemic awareness, or PPA, instruction works to enhance correct speech, improve understanding and application of accurate letter-to-sound correspondence, and strengthen spelling skills. Since skill-building involving phonemes is not a natural process, PPA instruction is especially important for children who have limited access and exposure to reading materials and who lack familial encouragement to read. Strategies that educators can implement include leading word and sound games, focusing on phoneme skill-building activities, and ensuring all activities focus on the fun, playful nature of words and sounds instead of rote memorization and drilling techniques.

<u>Deletion</u>

Phoneme deletion promotes the development of a child's phonemic awareness, which is part of developing their overall phonological awareness. Deletion involves having students take a word and delete a specific phoneme to create a new word. For example, a student might start with the word "groundhog". The teacher may ask the student to say the word without "hog". The student would say "ground." Deletion in an important step in literacy development and phonemic/phonological awareness, as it is yet another way for a child to manipulate and show mastery of language and literacy development.

Phonological & Phonemic Awareness Including Emergent Literacy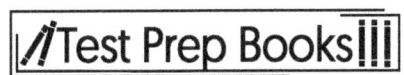

Substitution
Phoneme substitution, like phoneme deletion, helps to develop a child's phonemic and phonological awareness. Substitution is when a student take a word and substitutes (a) certain phonemes within the word with other phonemes, creating a new word. We looked at an example of this earlier. Take the word "cat." Substitute the /k/ sound (phoneme) with the /b/ sound (phoneme). In doing so, you get a new word, "bat." Substitution, like deletion, is another way for a child to manipulate and show mastery of language and literacy.

Develop Student's Expressive and Receptive Language Skills

English Literacy Development
English language literacy can be categorized into four basic stages:

- Beginning
- Early Intermediate
- Intermediate
- Early Advanced

Beginning Literacy
This stage is commonly referred to as **receptive language development**. Educators can encourage this stage in literacy development by providing the student with many opportunities to interact on a social level with peers. Educators should also consider starting a personal dictionary, introducing word flashcards, and providing the student with opportunities to listen to a story read by another peer, or as a computer-based activity.

Early Intermediate Literacy
When a child begins to communicate to express a need or attempt to ask or respond to a question, the child is said to be at the **early intermediate literacy stage**. Educators should continue to build vocabulary knowledge and introduce activities that require the student to complete the endings of sentences, fill in the blanks, and describe the beginning or ending of familiar stories.

Intermediate Literacy
When a child begins to demonstrate comprehension of more complex vocabulary and abstract ideas, the child is advancing into the **intermediate literacy stage**. It is at this stage that children are able to challenge themselves to meet the classroom learning expectations and start to use their newly acquired literacy skills to read, write, listen, and speak. Educators may consider providing students with more advanced reading opportunities, such as partner-shared reading, silent reading, and choral reading.

Early Advanced Literacy
When a child is able to apply literacy skills to learn new information across many subjects, the child is progressing toward the early **advanced literacy stage**. The child can now tackle complex literacy tasks and confidently handle much more cognitively demanding material. To strengthen reading comprehension, educators should consider the introduction to word webs and semantic organizers. Book reports and class presentations, as well as continued opportunities to access a variety of reading material, will help to strengthen the child's newly acquired literacy skills.

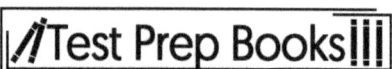 Phonological & Phonemic Awareness Including Emergent Literacy

Instructional Methods to Teach Beginning Readers Concepts about Print

Concepts of Print

Print awareness, the understanding that printed words carry meaning, aids reading development. Print awareness includes the understanding that:

1. **Words** are made of letters, spaces appear between words, and words make sentences.

2. **Print** is organized in a particular way (e.g., read from left to right and top to bottom, read from front to back, etc.), so books must be tracked and held accordingly.

3. Different types of print serve specific purposes (magazines, billboards, essays, fiction, etc.).

Print awareness provides the foundation on which all other literacy skills are built. It is often the first stage of reading development. Print awareness helps students develop skills such as word reading, reading comprehension, and letter-sound correspondence. For this reason, a child's performance on tasks relevant to their print awareness is indicative of the child's future reading achievement.

The following strategies can be used to increase print awareness in students:

1. An adult reads aloud to students or conducts shared reading experiences.. In order to maximize print awareness within the student, the reader should point out the form, function, orientation, and sounds of letters and words.

2. Utilize shared reading experiences as a tool for building one-to-one correspondence. **One-to-one correspondence** is the ability to match written letters or words to a spoken word when reading. This can be accomplished by pointing to words as they are read. This helps students make text-to-word connections. Pointing also aids **directionality**, or the ability to track the words that are being read.

3. *Use the child's environment.* To reinforce print awareness, teachers can make a child aware of print in their environment, such as words on traffic signs. Teachers can reinforce this by labeling objects in the classroom.

4. Instruct students about book organization during read-alouds. Students should be taught the proper orientation, tracking, and numbering conventions of books. For example, teachers can differentiate the title from the author's name on the front cover of a book.

5. *Let students practice.* Allowing students to practice book-handling skills with wordless, predictable, or patterned text will help to instill print awareness.

Return Sweep

Return sweeping refers to a reader moving their eyes from the end of one line on the right side of the page back to the left side of the page to begin a new line. The return sweep can be taught by modeling pointing to the words when reading to your child. Your child will learn to do this as they begin reading independently, and physically moving their finger from the end of one sentence to the beginning of the next will help train their eyes to follow this same process.

Phonological & Phonemic Awareness Including Emergent Literacy

Parts of a Book

It is important to teach a new reader the different parts of a book, as each part contains its own valid and useful information. While there are simpler ways to reduce this list, here is an extensive list of the different parts/components of a standard book.

(1) Front Matter

    (a) Title

    (b) Copyright information

    (c) Dedication (if applicable)

    (d) Table of Contents

    (e) Foreword (if applicable)

    (f) Acknowledgments

    (g) Preface or Introduction (if applicable)

    (h) Prologue (if applicable)

(2) Body Matter

    (a) This is the content of the book

(3) Back Matter

    (a) Epilogue (if applicable)

    (b) Appendix (if applicable)

    (c) Glossary (if applicable)

    (d) Bibliography (if applicable)

    (e) Index (if applicable)

    (f) Author's biography

Of course, depending on the type of book someone is reading, the information contained in the book will vary.

The Form and Function of Print

Fostering print awareness also entails making sure the reader understands what books are used for and how a book actually works. This means that the reader needs to know how to turn a page, how to navigate the page (numbers and chapters), and how to distinguish the different parts of the book.

Included in this is also making sure the reader knows that print is typically organized from left to right and that there should be spaces between words. In order to help a new reader develop stronger print awareness and understanding of the form and function of print, environmental intervention is

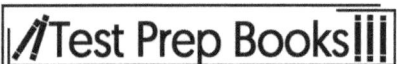

Phonological & Phonemic Awareness Including Emergent Literacy

necessary. This means that parents and peers and any other influential members in the reader's life should make it a point to point out print. They should not only point out print but also make it a point to point out the different forms within print (i.e. line spacing, capitalization, page layouts, etc.)

Identifying Upper-and Lowercase Letters in Various Fonts

Recognizing Uppercase and Lowercase Letters

Among the skills that are used to determine reading readiness, letter identification is the strongest predictor. **Letter recognition** is the identification of each letter in the alphabet. Letter recognition does not include letter-sound correspondences; however, learning about and being able to recognize letters may increase student motivation to learn letter sounds. Also, the names of many letters are similar to their sounds, so letter recognition serves as a gateway for the letter-sound relationships that are needed for reading to occur. Similarly, the ability to differentiate between uppercase and lowercase letters is beneficial in determining where a sentence begins and ends.

To be fluent in letter identification, students should be able to identify letter names in and out of context with automaticity. In order to obtain such familiarity with the identification of letters, students need ample experience, acquaintance, and practice with letters. Explicit instruction in letter recognition, practice printing uppercase and lowercase letters of the alphabet, and consistent exposure to printed letters are essential in the instruction of letter recognition.

Research has revealed that the following sequencing guidelines are necessary to effectively promote letter naming and identification:

1. The initial stage includes visual discrimination of shapes and curved lines.

2. Once students are able to identify and discriminate shapes with ease, then letter formations can be introduced. During the introduction of letter shapes, two letters that share visual (*p* and *q*) or auditory (/a/ and /u/) similarities should never be presented in back-to-back.

3. Next, uppercase letters are introduced. Uppercase letters are introduced before lowercase letters because they are easier to discriminate visually than lowercase letters. When letter formations are first presented to a student, their visual system analyzes the vertical, horizontal, and curved orientations of the letters. Therefore, teachers should use think-alouds when instructing how to write the shape of each letter. During think-alouds, teachers verbalize their own thought processes that occur when writing each part of a given letter. Students should be encouraged to do likewise when practicing printing the letters.

4. Once uppercase letters are mastered, lowercase letters can be introduced. High-frequency lowercase letters (*a, e, t*) are introduced prior to low-frequency lowercase letters (*q, x, z*).

5. Once the recognition of letters is mastered, students need ample time manipulating and utilizing the letters. This can be done through sorting, matching, comparing, and writing activities.

Practice Quiz

1. Which of the following terms refers to techniques that allow students to progress toward a greater level of understanding on an increasingly independent level?
    a. Discourse
    b. Differentiation
    c. Scaffolding
    d. Benchmarking

2. Which of the following statements about literacy development is true?
    a. Research shows that literacy development begins as early as 3 months of age.
    b. Between 3 months and 6 months, babies begin to study a speaker's mouth and listen closely to speech sounds.
    c. Between 6 months and 9 months, babies can generally recognize a growing number of commonly repeated words, utter simple words, respond appropriately to simple requests, and begin to attempt to group sounds.
    d. Between 9 months and 12 months, babies rapidly strengthen their communication skills, connecting sounds to meanings and combining sounds to create coherent sentences.

3. Receptive language development refers to which of the following stages of literacy?
    a. Beginning literacy
    b. Early intermediate literacy
    c. Intermediate literacy
    d. Early advanced literacy

4. While studying vocabulary, a student notices that the words circumference, circumnavigate, and circumstance all begin with the prefix circum–. The student uses her knowledge of affixes to infer that all of these words share what related meaning?
    a. Around, surrounding
    b. Travel, transport
    c. Size, measurement
    d. Area, location

5. What is a phoneme?
    a. A word
    b. A relationship between a letter and a sound
    c. An individual sound
    d. A consonant

See answers on next page

Answer Explanations

1. C: *Scaffolding* refers to techniques that allow students to progress toward a greater level of understanding on an increasingly independent level by incrementally increasing difficulty and independence. *Discourse* is a general term that refers to oral or written communication, so Choice A is incorrect. *Differentiation* refers to tailoring instructional methods and activities towards individual students or different levels. Therefore, Choice B is incorrect. Choice D is incorrect because *benchmarking* refers to setting measurable standards during the learning process.

2. B: Choice B is a correct statement about the generally accepted progression of normal literacy development. Choice A is incorrect because research indicates that literacy development begins from birth, and that from birth to 3 months of age, babies start recognizing the sounds of familiar voices, and this actually begins the early stages of literacy development. Choices C and D are incorrect because those skills start developing a bit later than stated, between 9 months and 12 months of age for Choice C, and in the toddler years for Choice D.

3. A: Receptive language development is a term used to describe the beginning literacy stage, during which children begin understanding the "input" of language. This means that they start developing the ability to connect words with their meanings and comprehend spoken language that others say or read.

4. A: The affix *circum–* originates from Latin and means *around or surrounding*. It is also related to other words that indicate something round, such as circle and circus. The rest of the choices do not relate to the affix *circum–* and are therefore incorrect

5. C: A phoneme is the smallest unit of sound (for example, the phonogram "ph" represents the phoneme /f/). Choice A, a word, is typically composed of multiple phonemes. Choice B refers to phonics, and Choice D is a subtype of phoneme.

Phonics and Decoding

Teaching Phoneme-Grapheme Correspondence

Phoneme-grapheme correspondence refers to a child's ability to recognize the correspondence between letter sounds and the visual representation of that letter. In order to teach phoneme-grapheme correspondences, the teacher could say the phoneme and have the student write the grapheme, either in the air or on paper. Prior to the student even being able to write, the teacher could say the phoneme and the student could just identify the grapheme from a small group. Another way to teach this correspondence, is having the student choose a graphic from a set of images that begins with the same sound said by the teacher.

Teaching Phonics Systematically, Explicitly, and Recursively

Teaching phonics **systematically** simply means that phonics instruction filters, categorizes, and prioritizes information for the student so as to prevent concept memory loss and inability to follow along. It provides a structure for teaching phonics rather than taking an unorganized approach.

Teaching phonics **explicitly** means that the teacher and student begin with the easiest sound within a word and then improve going forward. This means going from the single sound, then to patterns, then to syllables, and then, eventually to the entire word.

Teaching phonics explicitly has been proven, through research, to be more effective than teaching phonics implicitly, or **recursively**. Implicit phonics focuses more on teaching from the whole word to its parts, rather than from its parts to the whole word, as done with explicit phonics.

Teaching Common Phonics Patterns and Rules

Decoding and encoding are **reciprocal phonological skills**, meaning that their steps are opposite of each other.

Decoding is the application of letter-sound correspondences, letter patterns, and other phonics relationships that help students read and correctly pronounce words. Decoding helps students to recognize and read words quickly, increasing reading fluency and comprehension. The steps of the decoding process are as follows:

1. The student identifies a written letter or letter combination.

2. The student identifies the sound of that letter or letter combination.

3. The student understands how the word's different letters or letter combinations fit together.

4. The student verbally blends the letter and letter combinations together to form a word.

Encoding is the spelling of words. In order to properly spell words, students must be familiar with letter/sound correspondences. Students must be able to put together phonemes, digraphs or blends, morphological units, consonant/vowel patterns, etc. The steps of encoding are identified below:

1. The student understands that letters and sounds make up words.

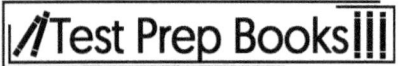

2. The student segments the sound parts of a word.

3. The student identifies the letter or letter combinations that correspond to each sound part.

4. The student then writes the letters and letter combinations in order to create the word.

Because the stages of decoding and encoding are reciprocal skills, phonics knowledge supports the development of reading and spelling. Likewise, the development of spelling skills reinforces phonics and decoding. In fact, the foundation of all good spelling programs is alignment with reading instruction and students' reading levels. Phonics instruction begins with simple syllable patterns and then progresses toward more complex patterns, the sounds of morphemes, and strategies for decoding multisyllabic words. Through this process, new vocabulary is developed. Sight word instruction should not begin until students are able to decode target words with automaticity and accuracy. Spelling is the last instructional component to be introduced.

Spelling development occurs in stages. In order, these stages are the pre-phonetic stage, the semiphonetic stage, the phonetic stage, the transitional stage, and the conventional stage. Each stage is explained below. Ways in which phonics and vocabulary development fit into the spelling stages are discussed. Instructional strategies for each phase of spelling are suggested.

Spelling development begins with the **pre-phonetic stage**, which is marked by an incomplete understanding of the alphabetic principle and letter-sound correspondences. During this stage, students participate in pre-communicative writing, which appears to be a jumble of letter-like forms rather than a series of discrete letters. Students' precommunicative writing samples can be used as informal

Phonics and Decoding

assessments of their understanding of the alphabetic principle and knowledge of letter-sound correspondences.

Pre-phonetic stage of spelling development

The pre-phonetic stage is followed by the **semiphonetic stage**, in which students understand that letters represent sounds. The alphabetic principle may be understood, but letter recognition may not yet be fully developed. In this stage, single letters may be used to represent entire words (e.g., *U* for *you*). Other times, multiple syllables within words may be omitted. Writing produced by students in this stage is still virtually unreadable. Teachers may ask students to provide drawings to supplement their writing to better determine what a student intended to write.

Semiphonetic stage of writing

The third stage in spelling development is the **phonetic stage**. In this stage, students have mastered letter-sound correspondences. Although letters may be written backward or upside down, phonetic spellers are able to write all of the letters in the alphabet. Because phonetic spellers have limited sight vocabulary, they will often spell irregular words incorrectly; however, these incorrectly spelled words may phonetically sound like the spoken word. Additionally, student writing becomes systematic. For example, students are likely to use one letter to represent a digraph or letter blend (e.g., *f* for /ph/).

Phonetic stage of writing

Spelling instruction of common consonant patterns, short vowel sounds, and common affixes or rimes can begin during the phonetic stage. Thus, spelling instruction during the phonetic stage coincides with the instruction of phonics and phonemic awareness that also occurs during this stage of development.

Word walls are advantageous during the phonetic stage because they provide visual groupings of words that share common consonant-vowel patterns or letter clusters. Students are encouraged to add words to each group. As a result, word walls promote strategic spelling, vocabulary development, common letter combinations, and common morphological units.

The **transitional stage** of spelling occurs when a student has developed a small sight vocabulary and a solid understanding of letter-sound correspondences. Thus, spelling dependence on phonology decreases. Instead, dependence on visual representation and word structure increases. As sight word

Phonics and Decoding

vocabulary increases during the transition stage, the correct spelling of irregular words will also increase. However, students may still struggle to spell words with long vowel sounds.

Transitional stage of spelling

Differentiation of spelling instruction often begins during the transitional stage. Instruction ought to be guided by data collected through informal observations and assessments. Depending on individual needs, lessons may include sight word recognition, morphology, etymology, reading, and writing. Students can begin learning about homophones during the transitional stage. **Homophones** are words that sound the same but have different spellings and meanings (e.g., *their* and *there*). Additionally, students should be expected to begin writing full sentences at the transitional stage. Writing reinforces phonics, vocabulary, and correct spelling of words.

The **conventional stage** comes last, occurring after a student's sight word vocabulary is well developed and the student is able to read fluently with comprehension. This stage occurs after a student's sight word vocabulary recognition is well developed and the student is able to read fluently and with comprehension. By this stage, students know the basic rules of phonics. They are able to deal with consonants, multiple vowel-consonant blends, homophones, digraphs, and irregular spellings. Due to an increase in sight word recognition at this stage, a conventional speller is able to recognize when a word is spelled incorrectly.

Conventional stage

It is at the conventional spelling stage that spelling instruction can begin to focus on content-specific vocabulary words and words with unusual spellings. In order to further reinforce vocabulary development of such content-specific words and apply phonic skills, students should be encouraged to use the correct spelling of such words within various writing activities.

For even the best conventional spellers, some words will still cause consistent trouble. Students can keep track of words that they consistently spell incorrectly or find confusing in word banks so they can isolate and eventually eliminate their individualized errors. Students can use their word banks as references when they come across a word with which they struggle. Students may also spend time consciously committing the words in their banks to memory through verbal or written practice.

Consonant Digraphs
Consonant digraphs are simply two or more consonants put together to represent a single sound. For example, in the word "tough," the "g" and "h" form "-gh," which can represent the sound /f/. A similar example would be the "p" and "h" in "digraph," also representing the sound /f/. Some other common consonant digraphs include: *ch, ck, kn, mb, ng, sh, th, wh,* and *wr.*

Blends
A **consonant blend** is similar to a consonant digraph in that it involves two or more consonants put together. However, blends differ in that each consonant that is "blended" still represents a different speech sound. For example, think of the "s" and "t" in "star." Or, you could think of the "c" and "l" in "clock". In this example, the "c" and "k" at the end would be an example of a consonant digraph.

Diphthongs
A diphthong is formed when two vowels combine to form a single syllable. The following chart shows common diphthongs. Each row contains similar sounds and examples of each type of diphthong.

Diphthong	Example	Diphthong	Example
"aw"	Straw, claw, law, saw, crawl	"au"	Haul, author, cause, pause, sauce
"ew"	Chew, blew, few, new, stew	"oo"	Food, shampoo, soon, room, balloon
"oi"	Point, join, coin, noise, spoil	"oy"	Boy, toy, joy, deploy, oyster
"ow"	Cow, how, brown, crown, flower	"ou"	House, cloud, round, ouch, found

Schwa Sound
The **schwa** sound is a sound that any vowel could make. The simplest way to characterize the schwa sound is to say that the vowel is making the short /u/ sound, or the /ŭ/ sound. This would sound like "uh." For example, words like *above*, *camel*, and *freedom* contain the short /u/ sound. In *above*, the "a" and the "o" make the schwa sound. In *camel*, the "e" makes the sound. In *freedom*, the "o" makes the sound.

Word Families
Word families are words that share the same pattern or feature. This could look like the same combinations or letters and/or having similar sounds. See the chart below for a representation of word families.

ake	ate	ick	est	ay	ight	ing	ock	uck	ice
awake	create	sick	best	away	light	bring	clock	duck	dice
brake	date	chick	rest	day	fight	swing	block	yuck	mice
make	late	kick	test	clay	night	ring	knock	truck	nice
snake	mate	lick	vest	okay	right	sting	shock	tuck	slice
rake	skate	trick	nest	play	sight	spring	dock	chuck	twice

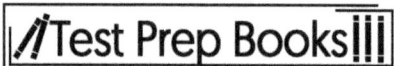

Phonics and Decoding

Morphological Analysis

Affixes
An **affix** is a letter or group of letters that can be added to a root word in order to change its meaning. There are **prefixes**, which are affixes added to the beginning of words; and there are **suffixes**, which are affixes added to the end of words. For example, in the word *transportable*, *-able* is the suffix.

Roots
The **root word** is the basic, original, and primary form of a word—what you get when you strip away the affixes. For example, in the word *transportable, port* would be the root word. It is the most basic and primary word that can be narrowed in the word *transportable*.

Base Words
Base words are very similar to root words. In fact, they are nearly indistinguishable. However, a base word is the word that can stand on its own. This is different from root words because not all root words may be able to hold significant meaning without additional letters. For example, in the word *transportable, transport* is the base word. It is not the root word because it is not simplified to the most basic and original form, however, it does still contain its meaning.

Syllable Types in Decoding Multisyllabic Words

Word-Analysis Skills
Phonics and decoding skills aid the analysis of new words. **Word analysis** is the ability to recognize the relationships between the spelling, syllabication, and pronunciation of new and/or unfamiliar words. Having a clear understanding of word structure, **orthography**, and the meaning of morphemes also aids in the analysis of new words.

However, not all words follow predictable patterns of phonics, morphology, or orthography. Such irregular words must be committed to memory and are called sight words.

Phonics skills, syllabic skills, structural analysis, word analysis, and memorization of sight words lead to word recognition automaticity. **Word recognition** is the ability to correctly and automatically recognize words in or out of context. Word recognition is a prerequisite for fluent reading and reading comprehension.

Reading Multisyllabic Words by Using Syllabication and Structural Analysis
Reading competence of multisyllabic words is accomplished through phonics skills that are accompanied with a reader's ability to recognize morphological structures within words. **Structural analysis** is a word recognition skill that focuses on the meaning of word parts, or morphemes, during the introduction of a new word. Therefore, the instruction of structural analysis focuses on the recognition and application of morphemes. **Morphemes** are word parts such as base words, prefixes, inflections, and suffixes. Students can use structural analysis skills to find familiar word parts within an unfamiliar word in order to decode the word and determine the definition of the new word. Identification and association of such word segments also aids the proper pronunciation and spelling of new multisyllabic words.

Similarly, learning to use phonics skills with more difficult words depends on a reader's ability to notice syllable structures within words that have more than one syllable. **Syllabic analysis**, or **syllabication**, is a word analysis skill that helps students split words into syllables. **Syllables** are phonological units that

Phonics and Decoding

contain a vowel sound. Students may be intimidated by long, multisyllabic words. Helping students break up multisyllabic words into morphological units (structural analysis) and phonological units according to syllable types makes longer words appear as a connected series of smaller words. The identified syllables can then be blended, pronounced, and/or written together as a single word. This helps students learn to decode and encode the longer words more accurately and efficiently with less anxiety. Thus, syllabic analysis leads to the rapid word recognition that is critical in reading fluency and comprehension.

The following table identifies the six basic syllable patterns that should be explicitly taught during syllabic instruction:

Basic Syllable Patterns		
Name of Syllable Type	Characteristics of Syllable Type	Examples
Closed	A syllable with a single vowel closed in by a consonant.	lab, bog, an
Open	A syllable that ends with a single vowel. Note that the letter *y* acts as a vowel.	go, me, sly
Vowel-Consonant-Silent *e*	A syllable with a single vowel followed by a consonant then *e*.	like, rake, note, obese
Vowel Teams	A syllable that has two consecutive vowels. Note that the letters *w* and *y* act as vowels.	meat, pertain, bay, toad, window
R-controlled	A syllable with one or two vowels followed by the letter *r*.	car, jar, fir, sir, collar, turmoil
Consonant *le (-al, -el)* Also called final stable	A syllable that has a consonant followed by the letters *le*, *al*, or *el*.	puddle, stable, uncle, bridal, pedal
Other final stable syllables	A syllable at the end of words can be taught as a recognizable unit such as *cious, age, ture, tion,* or *sion*.	pension, elation, puncture, stumpage, fictitious

Multisensory Approaches for Supporting Student Recognition of Nondecodable/Irregularly Spelled Words

While many words can be deciphered and spelled phonetically, that is, based on the sounds of their letters, non-decodable or irregular words cannot be read or spelled phonetically. Often, these words are taught as "**trick words**" or "**sight words**" to be recognized automatically as a whole word instead of as individual letter sounds. In the earliest grades, some sight words may be regular words that students can eventually decode with phonics (for example, it, can, not), and others are irregular words that cannot be easily decoded (for example, was, listen, though, once).

Traditionally, **non-decodable** or **irregular words** have been taught as whole words through visual memory and flashcards. However, not all students learn best this way. A **multisensory approach** provides alternative ways to learn by engaging other senses. Engaging different senses activates different parts of the brain, which makes content accessible for greater variety of learners.

Writing, tracing, or building irregular words helps to increase recall, particularly if the student names the letters while writing or placing them in the correct order. **Rainbow writing**, or repeatedly tracing over the letters in a word with different colors of pencils or crayons, provides variety and fun. So does writing words with different types of letters (for example, bubble letters or fancy letters). Writing need not be limited to paper, though. Other options include writing on white boards or chalkboards, writing in sand or shaving cream, and writing in the air with a pointer finger. Alternatively, words can be built with letters on various media including paper letters, rubber stamps, letter tiles, magnetic letters, letters written on cubes or blocks, or letter beads. Letters can also be created using based modeling clay, or even posable wax sticks.

Flash cards provide a repetitive visual review of irregular words. They can also be used to create interactive games that further reinforce learning in a more kinesthetic and interactive way. The games bingo, Memory Match, and Go Fish are all easy to set up, explain, and play.

Worksheets can help to reinforce learning of irregular words. Teachers can create coloring sheets that have words in different sections; each word corresponds to a particular color, as in a color-by-number drawing. Read It, Write It, Build It worksheets display an irregular word with spaces in which the student can write the word and also build it with paper letters, rubber stamps, or other media. Students should also be given the opportunity to read and construct sentences containing the irregular words.

When repeating words and their spellings, using different sounds and gestures can make them memorable. For example, say "g-o, go" while pointing away from yourself, or spell "w-h-a-t" and then draw out the question "whaaaat?" while raising your arms in a questioning posture and tilting your head to the side. Chanting is another vocal and auditory way to reinforce words through repetition. There are also educational songs available online that reinforce the learning of particular sight words.

Finally, students may benefit from kinesthetically engaging with irregular words. Ask a student to jump to the card containing a particular sight word among those laid out on the floor. Alternatively, you can write the words on sticky notes and place them on the wall; have students jump to tap the appropriate word. You can also lay the cards on a table and have students swat them with a fly swatter.

Practice Quiz

1. All EXCEPT which of the following are considered non-decodable sight words?
   a. None
   b. Who
   c. Runner
   d. Said

2. Which of the following statements is true regarding decoding and encoding?
   a. Decoding is the spelling of words.
   b. Encoding helps students to recognize and read words quickly.
   c. Encoding is the application of letter-sound correspondences, letter patterns, and other phonics relationships.
   d. Decoding and encoding are learned in opposite stages or steps.

3. Which of the following displays an INCORRECT matching of an orthographic pattern with an example of that pattern?
   a. Vowel-vowel digraph that have the same sound: player and jail
   b. Vowel-vowel digraph that have the same sound: read and speed
   c. Vowel-consonant digraphs with different sounds: foot and fool
   d. Vowel-consonant digraphs with different sounds: harm and have

4. Kimberly draws a picture of her family, and her instructor asks her to write what she drew on the line below the picture. She puts together a jumble of letter-like forms rather than a series of discrete letters. The instructor asks her what she wrote and she replies, "My family." Which stage of spelling development is Kimberly in?
   a. Pre-phonetic stage
   b. Semiphonetic stage
   c. Phonetic stage
   d. Conventional stage

5. A student is trying to read the word preferred. She first recognizes the word red at the end, then sounds out the rest of the word by breaking it down into pre, then fer, then red. Finally, she puts it together and says preferred. This student is displaying what attribute?
   a. Phonemic awareness
   b. Phonics
   c. Fluency
   d. Vocabulary

See answers on next page

Answer Explanations

1. C: The word runner is a decodable word because it follows the rules of phonics and is spelled phonetically. The other three choices are considered non-decodable sight words that students simply need to memorize because they are not spelled phonetically.

2. D: Choice D is correct because decoding and encoding are reciprocal phonological skills, meaning that the steps to each are opposite of one another. It is because of this reciprocal relationship that the development of phonics, vocabulary, and spelling are interrelated. The other answer choices are incorrect because they ascribe the wrong term to the given definition or skill.

3. D: Choice D is an incorrect match between *harm* and *have* are vowel-constant digraphs that have the same sound.

4. A: Kimberly is in the pre-phonetic stage of spelling because she formed a jumble of letter-like forms rather than a series of discrete letters. This indicates she has pre-communicative writing ability only. Her letter-sound correspondence is limited. In the semi-phonetic stage, she would have demonstrated a better understanding of the fact that letters represent sounds. She may have missed syllables in her words or used single letters to represent entire words, but she would have demonstrated letter formation and the alphabetic principle. The other choices list stages in which her spelling would be even further advanced.

5. B: Phonics is the ability to apply letter-sound relationships and letter patterns in order to pronounce written words accurately. Phonemic awareness is the understanding that words are comprised of a combination of sounds. Fluency is an automatic recognition and accurate interpretation of text. Vocabulary is the body of words that a person knows.

Vocabulary and Fluency

Build, Expand, and Use Expressive and Receptive Vocabulary

New vocabulary words should be chosen on the basis of how relevant they are to what students are learning and reading at the time. When choosing which words to teach, it may be helpful to consider a word's tier. Tier one words are used commonly in speech and usually learned through oral language. Tier two words are used in many subjects, and tier three words are specific to particular subjects. Generally, vocabulary words taught through literacy falls within tier two.

To teach a new vocabulary word, start by saying the word and having students repeat it. Ask students to reflect on and discuss whether they're familiar with the word or its meaning. When possible, link the word with previously learned words or concepts.

Work with students and use appropriate resources (such as dictionaries) to help them develop a definition that plainly captures meaning in a way that is accessible to them. Use a vocabulary word in a sentence and ask students to do the same. Display vocabulary words, their definitions, and even related pictures on a word wall or in a graphic organizer.

Next, read aloud or have students read a level-appropriate text that includes the new vocabulary words. If reading aloud, stop to point out the vocabulary words as you read them. Walk through your thinking process of decoding the word and remind students of its meaning in this context. If students are reading independently, have them find and highlight new vocabulary words and review their definitions before they read the text.

Reinforce the learning of new vocabulary words with games like bingo, charades, and Pictionary. Challenge students to use the new words as much as they can when they're talking and writing, and praise them when they do.

Teaching Vocabulary in Multiple Contexts

The key to embedding a vocabulary word in students' long-term memory is to expose them to the word multiple times in different contexts including various texts, images, audio, and multimedia. Teachers should use engaging and varied instruction to teach and reinforce new vocabulary words.

Maximize how often and in what ways students are exposed to vocabulary words by including definitions and examples as well as illustrations and anecdotes that make the words more memorable and meaningful for students. Gestures or miming can be used to physically engage students in the representation of a word. In addition to having the teacher represent the word in auditory, visual, and kinesthetic ways, it is particularly beneficial to have students make their own personal connections to the word, thereby maximizing the likelihood that they will remember its meaning. Encouraging students to think-pair-share with a partner can help to stimulate thinking. Other ways of encouraging students to make personal connections to words include using semantic maps to provide images, examples, synonyms, and even song lyrics or other attributes to help students categorize vocabulary words and connect them with prior knowledge. Alternatively, students can use sticky notes or pictures to add their visual or word-related (for example, synonyms, antonyms) impressions to a word wall.

It is important to vary the ways in which students practice their new vocabulary words. Flash cards with words on one side and definitions or related visuals on the reverse are helpful for students who learn through repetition. Alternatively, students can sort words into categories (for example, parts of speech; people, places, things; or categories of the students' choosing). Teachers can provide samples with vocabulary words used incorrectly and ask students to correct the mistakes. Finally, writing or speaking assignments in which students are tasked with correctly using new vocabulary words can also reinforce their learning.

Match an Instructional Method to Word Complexity

Texts should not be too hard or too easy for students. But how can teachers evaluate text complexity to ensure that they are giving their students appropriate materials? There are quantitative and qualitative methods of determining a text's level.

Quantitative measures attempt to objectively calculate the difficulty of a text. The most common quantitative measures are **readability formulas**, or mathematical equations that strive to calculate the difficulty of a text. **Fry's formula** is a common readability formula that requires teachers to count the number of sentences and syllables in three random passages of one hundred words each. They then average each number and chart the two numbers on a Fry graph. The **Fry graph** uses the numbers to produce a suggested grade level for the text. While this method is a useful tool for estimating a text's complexity, teachers should take it with a grain of salt; Fry's formula does not account for variation within grade levels and the text's qualitative factors.

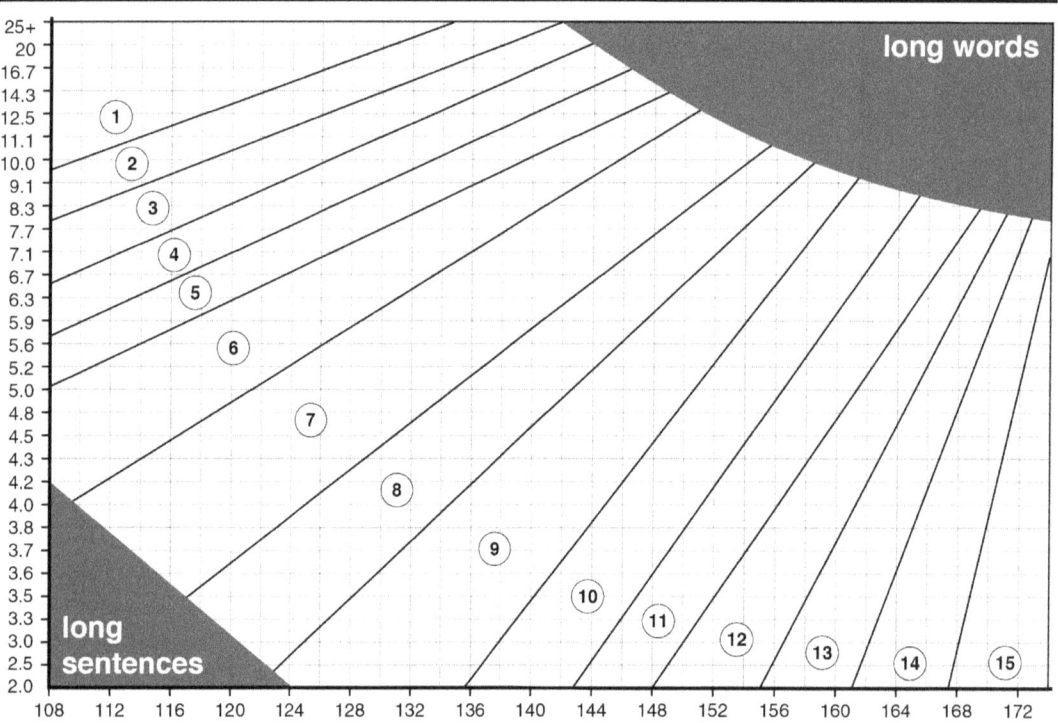

The other common quantitative measures are **Lexile text measures**. Like Fry's formula, these measures rate texts based on sentence length and word complexity. However, the Lexile method uses a database

Vocabulary and Fluency

of text rankings instead of having teachers do the math themselves. It also gives texts a numerical rating from 0L to 2000L (L stands for Lexile) instead of a grade level.

Qualitative measures identify subjective elements that affect the text's complexity. Below are some qualitative criteria that teachers can use to determine complexity.

- **Predictable structures** make texts easier to grasp, and they are especially useful in material intended for young children. For example, many fairy tales and children's books repeat questions and phrases. These predictable elements make the text less complicated, as children get into the pattern of the story and do not have to approach each repetition as an entirely new element.

- **Vocabulary** also determines a text's difficulty, and it cannot always be detected by quantitative measures. For example, the word "daft" consists of just one syllable, but it is clearly a more obscure word than "cat." However, Fry's formula would count the two words as the same level. Hence, teachers should skim the material to ensure the vocabulary is at an appropriate level. While texts should include some vocabulary words that will be new to students, an excess of new vocabulary renders reading so frustrating that students are likely to lose interest.

- Teachers should also consider the level of **background knowledge** required to understand a text. If easily learned background information is required (for example, basic historical context), teachers can present it to students before they begin to read a book. But if the background knowledge is complicated or far above the students' grade level, the book is not a good fit.

- Lastly, the **level of meaning** refers to how much abstract thought a text requires. Some texts only require students to understand the literal events of the book. More complex books, however, demand that students use abstract thought to make inferences and evaluate events. High levels of symbolism and abstract thought will be too difficult for younger students, while books that require only literal interpretation will likely seem boring to more mature students.

Teaching Word Solving

Context Clues

Reference materials are the most obvious way students can independently learn the definitions and pronunciations of new vocabulary terms.

When using **contextual strategies**, students are introduced to new words indirectly within a sentence or paragraph. Contextual strategies require students to infer the meaning of a word by utilizing semantic and contextual clues.

Appositives and parenthetical elements can be very effective contextual strategies. **Appositives** are words that define or add meaning to a term that directly precedes them. An example of a sentence that includes apposition is: "Strawberries, heart-shaped and red berries, are delicious when eaten right off of the vine." In this sentence, the definition of strawberries ("heart shaped and red berries") directly follows the term and is introduced with and closes with a comma. **Parenthetical elements** are specific types of appositives that add details to a term but not necessarily a definition. For example: "My cat, the sweetest in the whole world, didn't come home last night." In this sentence, the parenthetical element ("the sweetest in the whole world") further describes the cat but does not provide a definition of the word "cat."

Structural Analysis

Structural analysis skills are beneficial in the pronunciation of new words. When readers use **structural analysis**, they recognize affixes or roots as meaningful parts within a word. When a new word doesn't contain parts that are recognized by a student, the reader can use phonic letter–sound patterns to divide the word into syllables. The word parts can then be combined to yield the proper pronunciation.

Word maps are visual organizers that promote structural analysis skills for vocabulary development. They may require students to provide definitions, synonyms, antonyms, and pictures for given vocabulary terms. Alternatively, **morphological maps** may be used to relate words that share a common morpheme.

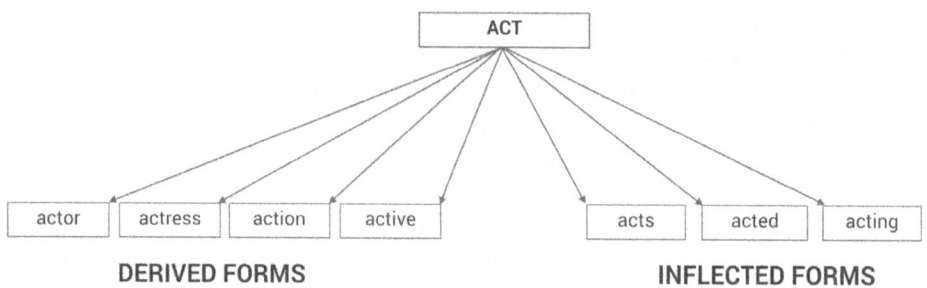

Vocabulary and Fluency

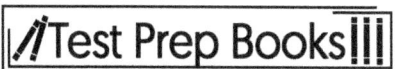

Similarly, **word webs** are used to compare and classify a list of words. Word webs show relationships between new words and a student's background knowledge. The main concept is in the center of the word web while secondary and tertiary terms stem off from it.

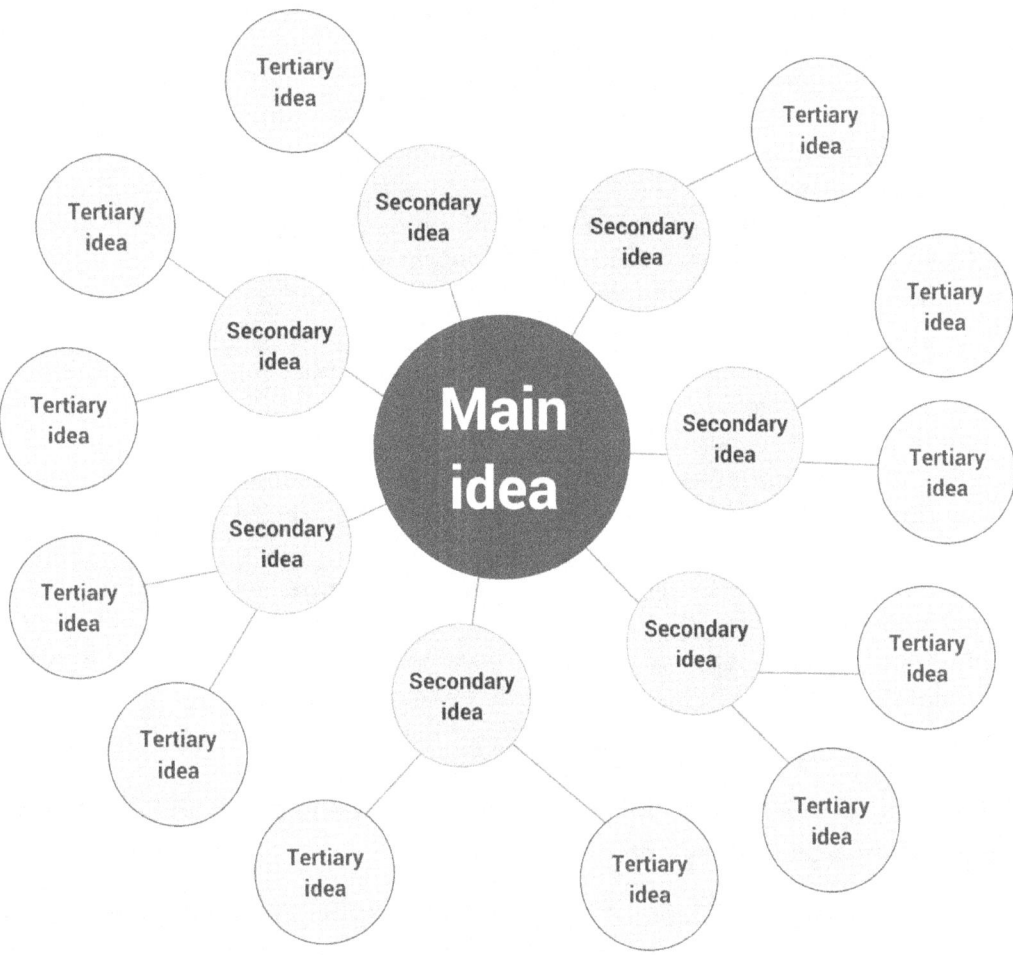

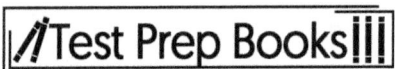

The table below identifies additional ways in which teachers can help students independently define unfamiliar words or words with multiple meanings:

Strategy	Examples
By Definition: Look up the word in a dictionary or thesaurus. Helps students realize that a single word can have multiple meanings.	Her favorite fruit to eat was a date. He went on a date with his girlfriend.
By Example: Invite students to offer their own examples, or to state their understanding following your own examples.	A myth is a story attempting to explain a natural phenomenon, such as the story of Prometheus to understand fire.
By Synonym: Understand that words have many different meanings. Some words are better synonyms than others.	She was very happy that day; her face was *radiant* with joy.
By Antonym: Teach student to look for words that have opposite meanings if the context of the sentence calls for its opposite.	Hannah was not happy that day; she was, in fact, very *depressed*.
By Apposition: **Apposition** is when the definition is given within the sentence.	The mango, a round, yellow, juicy fruit with an enormous seed in the middle, was ripe enough to eat.
By Origin: Identify Greek and Latin roots to figure out meanings of words.	In the word *hypertension*, the root "*hyper*" is a Greek word meaning "above" or "over."
By Context: Identifying what a word means by the surrounding text.	Water evaporates when it becomes hot, and the liquid turns into gas.

Guide Students to Understand a Wide Variety of Words through Direct Instruction and Independent Vocabulary Learning

All of the following strategies are best used together. To get the most out of a student's vocabulary learning, there must be common associations made, contextual strategies in place, and numerous opportunities to hear and connect with content-specific language. Rather than thinking of these as separate concepts, start trying to think about ways to integrate them and use them to reinforce each other and the student's learning.

Common

It's important to develop a nurture a student's understanding through **common** experiences. When a student is able to relate to something, an experience or memory perhaps, they then build a stronger connection with it, deepening their memory and understanding of it. With language and vocabulary, it works this same. If a student is able to make a common association with a new word, they are more likely to remember it. This is reinforced if that common association is shared among a group as well.

Contextual

As previously mentioned, when using **contextual strategies**, students are introduced to new words indirectly within a sentence or paragraph. Contextual strategies require students to infer the meaning of a word by utilizing semantic and contextual clues.

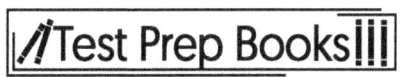

Vocabulary and Fluency

Content-Specific

Using common associations and contextual strategies help a student to learn **content-specific** terms and commit them to memory and understanding. As previously mentioned, there is immense benefit if common items or experiences can be associated with new terms, making the new terms more familiar and thus easier to retain. Additionally, if students are able to use their context clues to better understand a new word, then they can also apply this strategy to more content-specific language. Additionally, if the content is taught in a way that is relevant to the student's interest, they will be more likely to pick up on content-specific language. It is important as an instructor to use content-specific language whenever possible so as to build familiarity for the students hearing that language. An instructor must model the kind of language they want students to use.

Instructional Methods to Foster Students' Automaticity

Automatic Word Recognition, Accuracy, and Prosody for Reading Fluency

Word recognition occurs when students are able to recognize and read a word automatically and correctly. Phonics and sight word instruction help with the promotion of accurate and automatic word identification and recognition. Once students are able to readily identify and recognize words, then they can focus on the meaning of the text and development of reading comprehension skills.

Phonics instruction stresses letter-sound correspondences and the manipulation of phonemes. Through phonics instruction, students discover the different sounds of a spoken language and how a written language's letters and symbols relate to one another. It is through the application of phonics principles that students are able to decode words. When a word is **decoded,** the letters that make up the printed word are translated into sounds. When students are able to recognize and manipulate letter-sound relationships of single-syllable words, they are able to apply such relationships to decode more complex words. In this way, phonics aids reading fluency and reading comprehension.

Sight words, sometimes referred to as **high-frequency words**, are words that are used often but may not follow the regular principles of phonics. Sight words may also be defined as words that students are able to readily recognize and read without having to sound them out. Students are encouraged to memorize words by sight so their reading fluency is not deterred through the frequent decoding of regularly- occurring irregular words. In this way, sight word recognition aids reading fluency and reading comprehension.

Accuracy, Rate, and Prosody

In order to understand the objectives of RICA's Domain 3, the following three key indicators of reading fluency must be understood:

- **Accuracy** refers to the correct reading and pronunciation of words.

- **Reading rate** refers to the speed at which an individual reads within a given amount of time, often measured in words per minute.

- **Prosody** refers to the appropriate use of expression, intonation, emphasis, and tone when reading.

As word recognition increases, readers become less taxed with the interpretation of a text; thus, reading fluency and comprehension improve. When students read too quickly or too slowly for their skill level, they may lose reading comprehension. As accuracy and fluency increase, students begin to read aloud with appropriate prosody, and reading becomes a natural process.

Methods of Supporting Fluent Reading Behaviors

Phoneme Level

Phonemic awareness is the ability to understand the individual sounds (phonemes) that make up words. Being able to identify and manipulate phonemes is a foundational skill for those learning to read. Although phonemic awareness is auditory and does not directly involve reading, it is vital in establishing a strong connection to language.

By breaking words down into their smallest units, readers gain an essential understanding of how letters relate to sounds. Phonemic awareness is often used as a predictor for future success with reading. Once a student reaches the point of phonemic awareness, it is much easier to learn about phonics and the visual component of printed words. The student will be able to approach new words with the skills necessary to sound them out.

It is important for teachers to explicitly teach phonemes. There are 44 phonemes, which are composed of the 26 letters of the alphabet. In many cases, phonemes have multiple different **graphemes** (or spellings). Without strong instruction, it is not uncommon for students to struggle with understanding basic word structure, phonics, and reading. Thus, the phoneme level is crucial in supporting fluent reading behaviors and setting students up for success.

Word Level

Word level reading focuses on word recognition and word identification. **Word recognition** is the ability to correctly and automatically recognize words in or out of context. Word recognition is a prerequisite for fluent reading and reading comprehension. This process does not usually require any conscious strategy and shows that the words are easily accessible in the memory. **Word identification** is the ability to confront previously unknown words and decode them. This is done through the use of phonics, letter patterns, context clues, and sight words.

With practice, identified words will become recognizable words. Once words become recognizable and less focus is placed on decoding, students can focus on fluency and comprehension. In order to ensure a strong foundation for word recognition and word identification, teaching phonemic awareness and phonics first is key. Without these fundamentals, word-level development may prove challenging. Literacy development is more successful when each stage of learning is given adequate time and practice before moving on to the next.

Passage Level

Reading aloud has proven effective in strengthening reading fluency. Whisper-reading accompanied by teacher monitoring has also proven effective for students who do not yet display automaticity in their decoding skills. Timed reading of sight phrases or stories also improves fluency with respect to rate. During a **timed-reading** exercise, the number of words read in a given amount of time is recorded. Routinely administering timed readings and displaying the results in graphs and charts has been shown to increase student motivation.

Vocabulary and Fluency

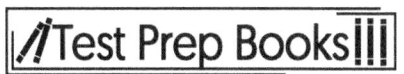

Timed-repeated readings, where a student reads and re-reads familiar texts in a given time, is a commonly used instructional strategy to increase reading speed, accuracy, and comprehension. Students read and re-read the passage until they reach their target rate.

Interrelations of Fluency, Vocabulary, and Comprehension

Fluency, vocabulary, and comprehension are all necessary components of developing successful reading skills. (They are the last three of the five essential components of reading instruction; the other two are phonemic awareness and phonics.) All three component skills—fluency, vocabulary, and comprehension—are interrelated and rely on one another. Let us review what each skill means. **Fluency** is the ability to read quickly and efficiently. Often times, fluent reading is compared to speaking in terms of speed and ease. Vocabulary refers to the knowledge of words, including their meaning and how they are used. Comprehension is the ability to understand what is being read. Understanding the meaning of what we are reading is the ultimate goal when learning how to read.

These three skills are all connected. Without a strong understanding of vocabulary, it will be difficult for a student to reach fluency. If a reader is pausing every sentence to look up a word or decode its meaning, that means that they are not reading smoothly or efficiently. The same goes for comprehension. Without knowing the meaning of the words, a student will struggle to understand the overall meaning of the writing. This could lead to misinterpreting the meaning and being unable to analyze texts. Difficulty with reading also affects also other types of schoolwork. For example, a long-form question on a science test may be difficult to comprehend without a solid understanding of vocabulary. Likewise, without fluency, it will be difficult for a student to comprehend what they are reading. The correlation is so strong that reading fluency is often used as a predictor for later comprehension skills. Once fluency is developed, readers can tackle longer texts at a higher level. This leads to an expanded vocabulary as they learn new words.

There are many strategies to assist readers with learning these skills. To help with vocabulary, teachers might consider putting up a word wall with words relevant to the students' reading levels. This promotes word consciousness (an awareness of words) and visual reinforcement. To help with fluency, oral reading repetition may prove useful. This allows students to become comfortable with the text and practice reading aloud. Reading orally helps students connect reading to their speech. This generally helps to improve the speed at which they read and the expression they give to the words. One way to improve reading comprehension is to ask students to summarize what they have just read. This will help them think critically about the text and reread until they are sure that they understand. Since all of these skills are interrelated, each one of these strategies will help with overall successful reading.

Practice Quiz

1. Which of the following is NOT true of word walls?
    a. They promote strategic spelling, vocabulary development, common letter combinations, and common morphological units.
    b. They help students sort words they know, want to know, and have learned.
    c. They are useful during the phonetic stage of spelling development.
    d. They group words that share common consonant-vowel patterns or letter clusters.

2. What is the study of what words mean in certain situations?
    a. Morphology
    b. Pragmatics
    c. Syntax
    d. Semantics

3. Which of the following is an essential component of effective fluency instruction?
    a. Spelling
    b. Writing
    c. Testing
    d. Practice

4. What are the three interconnected indicators of reading fluency?
    a. Phonetics, word morphology, and listening comprehension
    b. Accuracy, rate, and prosody
    c. Syntax, semantics, and vocabulary
    d. Word exposure, phonetics, and decodable skills

5. Which of the following about effective independent reading is NOT true?
    a. Students should read texts that are below their reading levels during independent reading.
    b. Students need to demonstrate fluency before reading independently.
    c. Students who do not yet display automaticity should whisper to themselves when reading aloud.
    d. Students who demonstrate automaticity in decoding should be held accountable during independent reading.

See answers on next page

Answer Explanations

1. B: Word walls are great tools for students as they learn to read, spell, and write. Because they help students pronounce unfamiliar words and provide visual contact with the word along with the auditory experience, they are particularly useful in the phonetic stage of spelling development. All of the statements given are correct except Choice *B*, which describes KWL charts typically used for reading.

2. B: Pragmatics is the study of what words mean in certain situations. Choice *A*, morphology, involves the structure and formation of words. Choice *C*, syntax, refers to the order of words in a sentence. Choice *D*, semantics, addresses the distinct meanings of words.

3. D: Practice is an essential component of effective fluency instruction. A student's accuracy and rate will likely increase if a teacher provides for them opportunities to learn words and use word-analysis skills.

4. B: Key indicators of reading fluency include accuracy, rate, and prosody. Phonetics and decodable skills aid fluency. Syntax, semantics, word morphology, listening comprehension, and word exposure aid vocabulary development.

5. A: Once students become fluent readers, independent reading can begin. Students who do not yet display automaticity may need to read out loud or whisper to themselves during independent reading time. Independent silent reading accompanied by comprehension accountability is an appropriate strategy for students who demonstrate automaticity in their decoding skills. Also, each student should be provided with a text that matches their reading level.

Comprehension of Literary and Informational Text

Support Students' Listening Comprehension

Listening comprehension is an important aspect of learning and a skill that can be developed and honed with time and effort. It can be enhanced by first activating students' background knowledge about the topic to be discussed; that way, they have some existing ideas to link the new information with. Letting them preview a few questions about the topic before listening gives them guidance on what information to focus on. Pausing throughout a listening exercise to ask students questions or having them summarize what they've heard thus far both also promote comprehension.

Students can practice listening comprehension through a variety of activities including conversing, following directions, and listening to stories. Teachers can help to build stamina in listening to stories by starting with reading shorter passages aloud and slowly increasing the amount students are expected to listen to and absorb.

Games are another great way to increase listening comprehension. The classic telephone game, in which each person takes a turn repeating to the next person what they heard from the previous person, is a great listening exercise. For another game, read a passage or story and then read it again with some changes to the details; have students identify the changes. In barrier games, two players sit on opposite sides of a visual barrier with identical materials in front of them. The players take turns describing how they are manipulating the materials, and the goal of is to have identical setups at the end of the game.

Listening Comprehension in Relation to Reading Comprehension

Listening and reading are both learned, receptive language skills that use the same areas of the brain. They are interconnected with writing and speaking, which are productive language skills, so working on any one of these skills also improves the others.

Gough and Tunmer's "simple view" of reading breaks it into two parts: **decoding** (recognizing and sounding out words) and **language comprehension** (the ability to understand language and the meaning of the words read). Everyone first learns to comprehend language by listening, a necessary base skill for reading and reading comprehension. Therefore, students can better understand complex language and connections by listening first rather than by reading first. Exposing them to different vocabulary words through listening also provides a foundation for reading comprehension once they are able to decode words.

Early reading education focuses on decoding, but as students become more fluent decoders, the goal shifts to learning through reading: the ability to make sense of what is read.

Reading comprehension is notably affected by both students' vocabulary and background knowledge. Listening exercises can be used to develop language skills that are critical to reading comprehension: using the text to understand and find meaning. Language skills include the ability to:

- Recall literal descriptions, facts, and details
- Decipher the meaning of unknown words using context in the passage
- Connect text using inferences and prior knowledge
- Identify the main idea
- Summarize text

Comprehension of Literary and Informational Text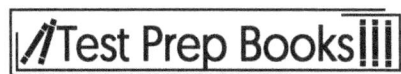

As younger students work to build their reading skills, non-print sources of information allow them to access technical language and topics better than they can through reading, and the non-print sources don't require them to expend mental energy decoding text. **Non-print sources** might include things like pictures or physical representations of associated words. The same is true of technical texts in older grades (for example, scientific writing). Therefore movies, performances, read-alouds, podcasts, and audiobooks are all good approaches to building listening comprehension, background knowledge, connections between existing and new knowledge, and vocabulary development that will strengthen students' reading comprehension. Students can also read along in a book or script while listening to an audio version, a strategy that enhances decoding and comprehension, particularly in struggling readers and English language learners. All these auditory activities can be enhanced by asking students to make predictions and summarize information; these tasks build the language skills that will further improve their reading comprehension.

Another activity for bridging listening comprehension and reading comprehension is to have students act out a story they've listened to. The teacher can assign parts and provide scripts. Students work individually and in groups to increase their fluency and comprehension by practicing reading their parts, with support from peers, teachers, or parents, as necessary. After several days of practice, the whole class can perform the story together with scripts in hand.

Support Students' Speaking and Listening Skills as they Discuss Texts

Students learn best when they can share their thoughts on what they've read or written and receive feedback from their peers and instructors. For writing, conferencing is frequently done in the revision stage. Through discussion, students are also able to enhance their listening and speaking skills. Conferences can be done in a one-on-one setting, typically between a student and instructor, or in a small group of students with guidance from the instructor. They are useful in that they provide an atmosphere of respect where a student can share their work and thoughts without fear of judgment. They increase motivation and allow students to explore a variety of topics and discussions. Conferences also allow the instructor to provide immediate feedback or prompt students for deeper explanations of their ideas. The most successful conferences have these characteristics:

- Have a set structure
- Focus on only a few points—too many are confusing or distracting
- Are solution based
- Allow students to both discuss their thoughts/works and receive/provide feedback for others
- Encourage the use of appropriate vocabulary
- Provide motivation and personal satisfaction or pleasure from reading and writing
- Allow a time where questions can be asked and immediately answered

Utilizing Background Knowledge

When students apply personal experiences to their reading, they exhibit **background knowledge**. They can recall the characteristics of other texts and apply their prior literary experiences to the new curriculum. The capability to retain and convey previous knowledge is representative of **reading fluency**; fluent readers are able to retain what they have read and quickly analyze texts. Fluency is usually an effect of reading often.

Background knowledge, or knowledge related to a text's topic, comes from readers' experiences as well as what they have learned by reading and listening. It allows readers to make connections that enhance

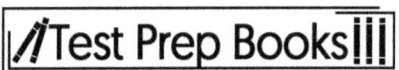

their ability to read, summarize, decipher word meaning, and comprehend the text. It also provides the information necessary to make inferences about meaning by using knowledge to build on the information explicitly provided in the text without getting lost in supportive details. Finally, background knowledge helps readers interpret literary devices like metaphors and idioms, and it helps them interpret increasingly technical, subject-specific topics in informational texts.

Readers' growth and development therefore critically rely on building background knowledge and activating it. Building background knowledge is not simply teaching students facts; instead, it involves strategically building interconnected webs of concepts that promote future learning. It's important for teachers to be aware of the diverse backgrounds of their students before having them read a book. This can help them identify areas of background knowledge that should be supplemented before reading.

One way to build and activate background knowledge across the curriculum is to give students time to read about and conduct in-depth research on a single topic using a variety of media. Teachers can pair fiction and nonfiction books on the same topic. Various media can be used to build and activate students' knowledge of different settings and cultures. Videos and virtual field trips can expose children to information that they will build on while reading a book set in an unfamiliar place or culture.

Activating students' background knowledge before they read a text helps them make connections to what they already know about a topic. One pre-reading strategy that works well with books that have many illustrations is a **picture walk**. Before reading, teachers draw students' attention to the cover, read the title aloud, and asking them to say what the story might be about. Flipping through the pages and stopping at illustrations, the teacher can ask questions about characters, plot, setting, and predictions (for example, "Who is this character?" "Where does the story take place?" "What do you think will happen next?") Picture walks activate background knowledge while also providing context that allows students to better decode vocabulary words.

Before and during reading, teachers can model behaviors that encourage students to make connections between what they are reading and their past experiences (text-to-self), other things they have read (text-to-text), and what they know about the world (text-to world). Students may share these connections verbally or through writing or drawing. While displaying the cover of a book, the teacher may say aloud, "This reminds me of the time I..." or "This book reminds me of the one we read...."

Methods for Teaching Comprehension

Reading comprehension involves the reader's use of prior knowledge, experience activation, prediction, text decoding, summarizing, and identification of the text's purpose to construct an understanding of the text's meaning.

Activating background knowledge before reading a new book can help students to recognize and decode new vocabulary words. Ask students to predict what might happen in the reading based on the title, cover art, and illustrations (if there are illustrations). Ask them to relate their ideas to their own experiences to further activate their background knowledge.

Comprehension is best achieved with fluent reading. Phonics skills and decoding ability both affect fluency, as does vocabulary knowledge. Students should be reading books at the appropriate level, which means the level at they can read at least 90 percent of the words; harder texts disrupt the flow of their reading, which can interfere with comprehension. Having students slow down their reading speed improves reading comprehension by giving them more time to process what they're reading. Reading aloud slows their pace and gives them auditory feedback. Further, rereading familiar texts facilitates decoding, enabling the student to read quickly and smoothly, which facilitates comprehension.

Discussion, or verbal processing, of text before, during, and after reading helps students to remember what they've read and create meaning and connections that enhance comprehension. Ask guided questions about what is happening in the book, what might happen next, and how the book relates to the students' experiences or other books they've read. Similarly, teach students to pause and monitor their understanding of texts that they read independently, and teach them to reread sections that they don't understand. Using a journal or sticky notes, they can write down questions they have and words they don't understand. They can enhance understanding by defining vocabulary words they don't know and restating a passage in their own words, either independently or in a think-pair-share activity with a peer. They can also use what they've learned to predict what will happen next in the story and then read on to see if their prediction was accurate. Another way to reinforce understanding while reading is to ask students to create a mental picture of the story.

Graphic organizers can also be used as tools to enhance comprehension; they do this by organizing information and highlighting main ideas and relationships in a text. For example, **storyboards** show the order of events in a book, flow charts show cause-and-effect relationships among events in a story, and **Venn diagrams** compare and contrast. **KWL charts** (the acronym stands for *know, want, learn*) encourage the students to identify what they know about a topic (background knowledge), what they want to know about it, and what they've learned from reading a passage. Older students can be introduced to a variety of graphic organizers and then encouraged to use the type that works best for them.

After reading a story, students should be able to summarize it, discerning which information is important enough to include among the main ideas. Using **a five-finger retell activity** is another way to summarize; the five fingers are associated with five aspects of the text: characters, setting, plot, ending, and favorite part. Having students identify what happened in the beginning, middle, and end is another. Comprehension questions (who, what, where, why, how) also help to gauge students' understanding after reading and assist them in making meaning of the text. Another tool is to have students write their own comprehension questions, which indicates whether they were able to accurately pull the main ideas from the text.

To accommodate students of various learning styles, teachers can vary the medium through which students exhibit their understanding of a text. Nontraditional media include comic strips, collages, skits, alternate endings, trivia, illustrated timelines, and oral presentations.

Using Metacognition for Comprehension and Analysis

Metacognitive strategies ask the student to decode text passages. In part, they require the student to preview text, be able to recognize unfamiliar words, then use context clues to define them for greater understanding. In addition, meta-cognitive strategies in the classroom employ skills such as being able to decode imagery, being able to predict, and being able to summarize. If a student can define unfamiliar vocabulary, make sense of an author's use of imagery, preview text prior to reading, predict outcomes during reading, and summarize the material, he or she is achieving effective reading comprehension. When approaching reading instruction, the teacher who encourages students to use phrases such as *I'm noticing, I'm thinking,* and *I'm wondering* is teaching a meta-cognitive type strategy.

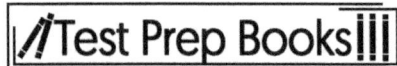

Comprehension of Literary and Informational Text

Pre-Reading Strategies

Pre-reading strategies are important, yet often overlooked. Non-critical readers will often begin reading without taking the time to review factors that will help them understand the text. Skipping pre-reading strategies may result in a reader having to re-address a text passage more times than is necessary. Some pre-reading strategies include the following:

- Previewing the text for clues
- Skimming the text for content
- Scanning for unfamiliar words in context
- Formulating questions on sight
- Making predictions
- Recognizing the need for prior knowledge

Before reading a passage, a reader can enhance their ability to comprehend material by previewing the text for clues. This may mean making careful note of any titles, headings, graphics, notes, introductions, important summaries, and conclusions. It can involve a reader making physical notes regarding these elements or highlighting anything they think is important before reading. Often, a reader will be able to gain information just from these elements alone. Of course, close reading is required in order to fill in the details. A reader needs to be able to ask what they are reading about and what a passage is trying to say. The answers to these general questions can often be answered in previewing the text itself.

It's helpful to use pre-reading clues to determine the main idea and organization. First, any titles, sub-headings, and chapter headings should be read, and the test taker should make note of the author's credentials if any are listed. It's important to deduce what these clues may indicate as it pertains to the focus of the text and how it's organized.

During pre-reading, readers should also take special note of how text features contribute to the central idea or thesis of the passage. Is there an index? Is there a glossary? What headings, footnotes, or other visuals are included and how do they relate to the details within the passage? Again, this is where any pre-reading notes come in handy, since a test taker should be able to relate supporting details to these textual features.

Next, a reader should **skim** the text for general ideas and content. This technique does not involve close reading; rather, it involves looking for important words within the passage itself. These words may have something to do with the author's theme. They may have to do with structure—for example, words such as *first, next, therefore*, and *last*. Skimming helps a reader understand the overall structure of a passage and, in turn, this helps them understand the author's theme or message.

From there, a reader should quickly **scan** the text for any unfamiliar words. When reading a print text, highlighting these words or making other marginal notation is helpful when going back to read text critically. A reader should look at the words surrounding any unfamiliar ones to see what contextual clues unfamiliar words carry. Being able to define unfamiliar terms through contextual meaning is a critical skill in reading comprehension.

A reader should also *formulate any questions* they might have before conducting close reading. Questions such as "What is the author trying to tell me?" or "Is the author trying to persuade my thinking?" are important to a reader's ability to engage critically with the text. Questions will focus a reader's attention on what is important in terms of main idea and supporting details.

Comprehension of Literary and Informational Text

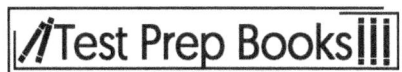

Along with formulating questions, it is helpful to make predictions of what the answers to these questions and others will be. **Making predictions** involves using information from the text and personal experiences to make a thoughtful guess as to what will happen in the story and what outcomes can be expected.

Last, a reader should recognize that authors assume readers bring a *prior knowledge* set to the reading experience. Not all readers have the same experience, but authors seek to communicate with their readers. In turn, readers should strive to interact with the author of a particular passage by asking themselves what the passage demands they know during reading. This is also known as making a text-to-self connection. If a passage is informational in nature, a reader should ask "What do I know about this topic from other experiences I've had or other works I've read?" If a reader can relate to the content, they will better understand it.

All of the above pre-reading strategies will help the reader prepare for a closer reading experience. They will engage a reader in active interaction with the text by helping to focus the reader's full attention on the details that they will encounter during the next round or two of critical, closer reading.

Strategies During Reading

After pre-reading, a test taker can employ a variety of other reading strategies while conducting one or more closer readings. These strategies include the following:

- Clarifying during a close read
- Questioning during a close read
- Organizing the main ideas and supporting details
- Summarizing the text effectively

A reader needs to be able to **clarify** what they are reading. This strategy demands a reader think about how and what they are reading. This thinking should occur during and after the act of reading. For example, a reader may encounter one or more unfamiliar ideas during reading, then be asked to apply thoughts about those unfamiliar concepts after reading when answering test questions.

Questioning during a critical read is closely related to clarifying. A reader must be able to ask questions in general about what they are reading and questions regarding the author's supporting ideas. Questioning also involves a reader's ability to self-question. When closely reading a passage, it's not enough to simply try and understand the author. A reader must consider critical thinking questions to ensure they are comprehending intent. It's advisable, when conducting a close read, to write out margin notes and questions during the experience. These questions can be addressed later in the thinking process after reading and during the phase where a reader addresses the test questions. A reader who is successful in reading comprehension will iteratively question what they read, search text for clarification, then answer any questions that arise.

A reader should **organize** main ideas and supporting details cognitively as they read, as it will help them understand the larger structure at work. The use of quick annotations or marks to indicate what the main idea is and how the details function to support it can be helpful. Understanding the structure of a text passage is sometimes critical to answering questions about an author's approach, theme, messages, and supporting details. This strategy is most effective when reading informational or nonfiction texts. Texts that try to convince readers of a particular idea, that present a theory, or that try to explain difficult concepts are easier to understand when a reader can identify the overarching structure at work.

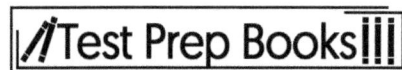

Comprehension of Literary and Informational Text

<u>Post-Reading Strategies</u>

After completing a text, a reader should be able to **summarize** the author's theme and supporting details in order to fully understand the passage. Being able to effectively restate the author's message, sub-themes, and pertinent, supporting ideas will help a reader gain an advantage when addressing standardized test questions.

A reader should also evaluate the strength of the predictions that were made in the pre-reading stage. Using textual evidence, predictions should be compared to the actual events in the story to see if the two were similar or not. Employing all of these strategies will lead to fuller, more insightful reading comprehension.

Guiding Students' Self-selection of Appropriate Texts

Students who engage in independent reading are able to read, retain, and analyze the text that they have read completely independent of outside aid. It also allows them to feel as if they had a choice in picking their own text to read, instead of the feeling that it has been chosen for them. **Reflective reading** is the ability to absorb text with a sense of analysis in mind. Here are some examples of questions students can ask themselves while engaged in reflective reading:

- What am I reading?
- Why am I reading this?
- What is the author trying to tell me?
- Why is this character acting in a certain way?

Encouraging independent and reflective reading is dependent on the type of literature instructors choose to introduce in their classrooms. Culture, race, age, and reading level are all very important characteristics to keep in mind when choosing texts to have in the classroom for independent readers. If some students are ELLs, acquire some texts that are bilingual or ELL-appropriate. Choose authors with various ethnic backgrounds rather than the most popular books at the time. Find authors who have similar cultures to the students in the classroom. Choose difficult books for your advanced students and appropriate books for the students who still struggle with reading. Students will have greater motivation to read and understand the language if they can relate to the message of the text.

Selecting Instruction, Tasks, and Materials

The classroom must be a place that emphasizes respect for all individuals as well as collaboration to achieve a successful learning environment. In addition to teaching reading skills, the instructor is expected to be a model of tolerance and inclusiveness for all students, thus encouraging them to be open-minded toward others. In the United States, it is likely that instructors will have students from a broad range of cultural and linguistic backgrounds. Obviously, these students must be made to feel welcome, and any linguistic difficulties they have should be treated as simply another step in the learning process, not as a result of their background. Any difficulty is an opportunity for the whole class to learn and grow.

Encouraging polite and respectful behavior is key. An instructor does not necessarily need to explain polite behavior, but rather should serve as a role model for the class. When addressing students' issues, the teacher should be sensitive to how they feel and be encouraging no matter their religious or ethnic background. It is also important to monitor how students act and respond to one another. Proper language and behavior should be enforced when necessary, and rude, insensitive language or behavior

Comprehension of Literary and Informational Text

must be addressed and corrected. Teachers should simultaneously emphasize diversity, equality, and respect for all. When disrespect occurs, steps should be taken to ensure that it is not repeated. It is important to remember that behaviors and lessons in early learners will inform how children grow and mature.

Reading and writing activities can also provide lessons in respect and collaboration. For instance, students can do group work on a text that discusses respectful behavior. Other lessons can look at readings from different cultures to expand the students' appreciation and interest in diversity.

Reading aloud is one of the best things teachers can do with students. It helps improve their language skills, their ability to identify story elements, and their overall desire to read. Reading culturally relevant, high-quality texts aloud enables children to see themselves represented in the story. Students are also more likely to memorize key elements of the stories when they can make personal connections to them.

Use of Graphic and Semantic Organizers to Support Comprehension

Make Lessons Visual by Using Graphic Organizers

Visual aids are another helpful tool when scaffolding; they can help students develop creativity and work with others to assist collaboratively in each other's creativity and ideas. **Graphic organizers** include webs, Venn diagrams, story boards, KWL charts, spider maps, and charts, all of which help students organize information and develop higher-level thinking.

Diagrams and graphic organizers provide students with visual clues to contrast and compare word meanings. From organizational charts and mind maps to Venn diagrams and more, visual aids help students readily see and analyze the similarities and differences in various word meanings.

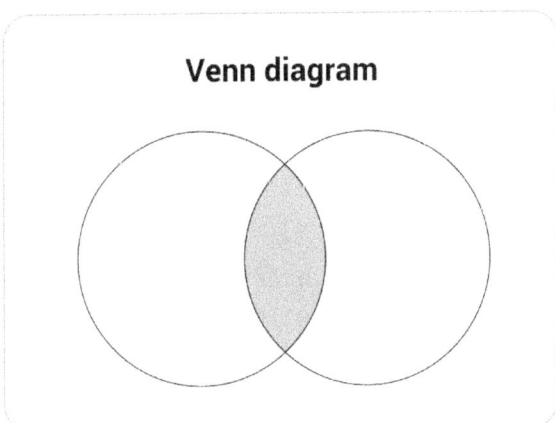

Semantic Organizers

To strengthen reading comprehension, educators should consider the introduction to word webs and **semantic organizers**.

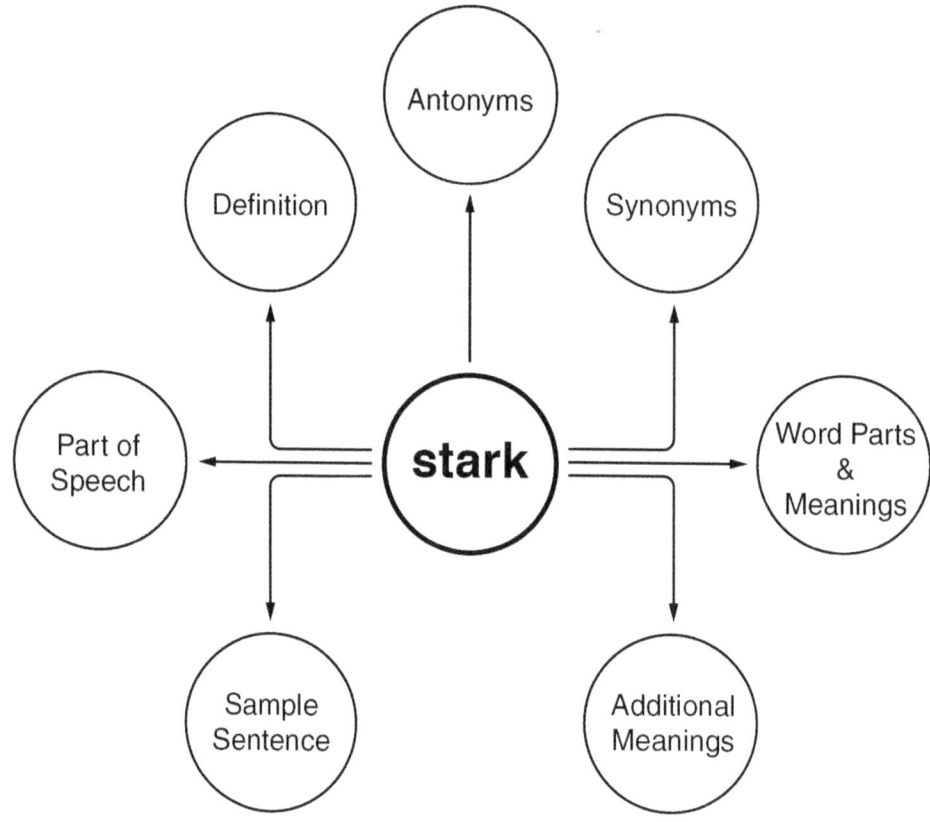

Genres, Structures, and Features of Literary Texts

Classifying literature involves an understanding of the concept of genre. A **genre** is a category of literature that possesses similarities in style and in characteristics. Based on form and structure, there are four basic genres.

Poetry
Poetry is fiction in verse that has a unique focus on the rhythm of language and focuses on intensity of feeling. It is not an entire story, though it may tell one; it is compact in form and in function. Poetry can be considered as a poet's brief word picture for a reader. **Poetic structure** is primarily composed of lines and stanzas. Together, poetic structure and devices are the methods that poets use to lead readers to feeling an effect and, ultimately, to the interpretive message.

Prose
Prose consists of fictional works written in standard form with a natural flow of speech and without poetic structure. Fictional prose primarily utilizes grammatically complete sentences and a paragraph structure to convey its message.

Drama
Drama is fiction that is written to be performed in a variety of media, intended to be performed for an audience, and structured for that purpose. It might be composed using poetry or prose, often straddling the elements of both in what actors are expected to present. Action and dialogue are the tools used in

Comprehension of Literary and Informational Text

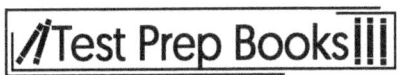

drama to tell the story. **Comedy** is any drama designed to be funny or lighthearted. **Tragedy** is any drama designed to be serious or sad.

Literary Nonfiction

Literary nonfiction is prose writing that is based on current or past real events or real people and includes straightforward accounts as well as those that offer opinions on facts or factual events. The exam distinguishes between **literary nonfiction**—a form of writing that incorporates literary styles and techniques to create factually-based narratives—and informational texts. Nonfiction has the following subgenres:

- **Informational Text:** This is text written to impart information to the reader. It may have literary elements such as charts, graphs, indexes, glossaries, or bibliographies.

- **Persuasive Text:** This is text that is meant to sway the reader to have a particular opinion or take a particular action.

- **Biographies and Autobiographies:** These texts that tells intimate details of someone's life. If an author writes the text about someone else, it is a **biography**. If the author writes it about himself or herself, it is an **autobiography.**

- **Communicative text:** This is text used to communicate with another person. It includes such texts as emails, formal and informal letters, and social media posts. This content often consists of two-sided dialogue between people.

Story Elements

There is no one, final definition of what **literary elements** are. They can be considered features or characteristics of fiction, but they are really more of a way that readers can examine a text for the purpose of analysis and understanding the meaning. The elements contribute to a reader's literary interpretation of a passage as to how they function to convey the central message of a work. The most common literary elements used for analysis are presented below.

Point of View

The **point of view** is the position the narrator takes when telling the story in prose. If a narrator is incorporated in a drama, the point of view may vary; in poetry, point of view refers to the position the speaker in a poem takes.

First Person

The **first-person point of view** is when the writer uses the word *I* in the text. Poetry often uses first person, e.g., William Wordsworth's "I Wandered Lonely as a Cloud." Two examples of prose written in first person are Suzanne Collins's *The Hunger Games* and Anthony Burgess's *A Clockwork Orange*.

Second Person

The **second person point of view** is when the writer uses the pronoun *you*. It is not widely used in prose fiction, but as a technique, it has been used by writers such as William Faulkner in *Absalom, Absalom!* and Albert Camus in *The Fall*. It is more common in poetry—e.g., Pablo Neruda's "If You Forget Me."

Third Person

Third person point of view is when the writer utilizes pronouns such as him, her, or them. It may be the most utilized point of view in prose as it provides flexibility to an author and is the one with which

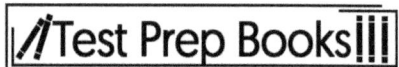

readers are most familiar. There are two main types of third person used in fiction. **Third person omniscient** uses a narrator that is all-knowing, relating the story by conveying and interpreting thoughts/feelings of all characters. In **third person limited**, the narrator relates the story through the perspective of one character's thoughts/feelings, usually the main character.

Plot
The **plot** is what happens in the story. Plots may be singular, containing one problem, or they may be very complex, with many sub-plots. All plots have an exposition, a conflict, a climax, and a resolution. The **conflict** drives the plot and is something that the reader expects to be resolved. The plot carries those events along until there is a resolution to the conflict.

Tone
The **tone** of a story reflects the author's attitude and opinion about the subject matter of the story or text. Tone can be expressed through word choice, imagery, figurative language, syntax, and other details. The emotion or mood the reader experiences relates back to the tone of the story. Some examples of possible tones are humorous, somber, sentimental, and ironic.

Setting
The **setting** is the time, place, or set of surroundings in which the story occurs. It includes time or time span, place(s), climates, geography—man-made or natural—, or cultural environments Emily Dickinson's poem "Because I could not stop for Death" has a simple setting—the narrator's symbolic ride with Death through town towards the local graveyard. Conversely, Leo Tolstoy's *War and Peace* encompasses numerous settings within settings in the areas affected by the Napoleonic Wars, spanning from 1805 to 1812.

Characters
Characters are the story's figures that assume primary, secondary, or minor roles. **Central or major characters** who are those integral to the story—the plot cannot be resolved without them. A central character can be a **protagonist** or hero. There may be more than one protagonist, and they don't always have to possess good characteristics. A character can also be an **antagonist**—the force against a protagonist.

Character development is when the author takes the time to create dynamic characters that add uniqueness and depth to the story. **Dynamic characters** are characters that change over the course of the plot's timeline. *Stock* characters are those that appear across genres and embrace stereotypes—e.g., the cowboy of the Wild West or the blonde bombshell in a detective novel. A **flat character** is one that does not present a lot of complexity or depth, while a *rounded* character does. Sometimes, the **narrator** of a story or the **speaker** in a poem can be a character—e.g., Nick Carraway in F. Scott Fitzgerald's *The Great Gatsby* or the speaker in Robert Browning's "My Last Duchess." The narrator might also function as a character in prose, though not be part of the story—e.g., Charles Dickens's narrator of *A Christmas Carol*.

Literary Devices

Figurative Language
Figurative language includes using devices such as simile, metaphor, hyperbole, personification, or allusion, to name a few, to enhance one's writing. **Creative writing** tends to employ more non-literal expressions than academic or informative writing. Educators should give students ample time to

Comprehension of Literary and Informational Text

experiment with different kinds of figurative language, especially when switching from creative to more academic writing.

Figurative language can be used to give additional insight into the theme or message of a text by moving beyond the usual and literal meaning of words and phrases. It can also be used to appeal to the senses of readers and create a more in-depth story. This is often seen in more descriptive writing.

It is also considered a rhetorical device in that figurative language is used to play on the *meanings* of words as well as the *sounds* of words. These kind of literary devices are more likely found in poetry but may also be found in non-fiction writing like speeches.

Nuance of Words

Reading material will grow more technical and complex between kindergarten and grade 6. Some students will adapt well to the new material, and others will struggle a bit with the nuances. The following are some research-based rereading practices to engage students who are having trouble understanding complicated texts.

Instructors can ask their students **text-dependent questions**, which require students to go back and reread the text in order to find answers. After diving deeper into the text, students should be able to craft thoughtful answers to the instructors' questions. Some examples of text-dependent questions are those that ask the meanings of words, the writer's point of view, and the purpose of the text.

Annotation, or the practice of highlighting or marking parts of the writing that seem important, also requires careful reading. Teachers can help students do this by telling them what concepts to look for in the writing. You could provide a helpful annotation worksheet, which lists what readers should look out for. Students could also write questions about parts of the text that need clarifying.

Annotation can also be used to deconstruct grammatically complex sentences. To do this, students can be asked to identify the sentence that gives them trouble and identify the nouns, verbs, adjectives, and so forth, by circling them. Then, ask them to identify the subject and verb. See if they can infer from the surrounding text what difficult words mean. If they can't, they can look them up.

Educators can also reread the text with the students and ask them what they think it means. More than likely, they will interpret it differently. Having them write down their perspectives and then read them aloud is an exercise that could spark in-class conversation. Teachers should use this opportunity to encourage collaboration between students. Breaking students into groups and giving them text-dependent questions is another exercise that will help spark discussion.

All of these strategies are effective at deciphering complex writing. Use them to encourage intentional reading and group communication.

Alliteration

Alliteration refers to the repetition of the first sound of each word. Alliteration can be used to build emotion in a peace, to cause the reader to slow down, or to add rhythm and structure to a piece. Recall Robert Burns' opening line:

> My love is like a red, red rose

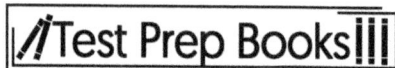

This line includes two instances of alliteration: "love" and "like" (repeated L sound), as well as "red" and "rose" (repeated R sound). Next, assonance refers to the repetition of vowel sounds, and can occur anywhere within a word (not just the opening sound). Here is the opening of a poem by John Keats:

> When I have fears that I may cease to be
>
> Before my pen has glean'd my teeming brain

Strategies for Supporting Readers as they Construct Literal and Inferential Meaning

Literal Comprehension

Literal comprehension refers to the reader's ability to understand the actual meaning of texts. This is not meant to be complicated. It means literally understanding the facts, setting, plot, etc. of what is being read.

To bolster literal comprehension, show students how to ask pertinent questions. When they are reading stories, children should learn to ask who the characters are, what happened, where the story is taking place, and in what order the events occurred.

Inferential Comprehension

Inferential comprehension requires students to understand the hidden context or unstated meaning of a text. They should be able to explain why an action occurred and what they think will happen next.

When it comes to inferential comprehension, children need to recall the facts that occurred in the story and what those facts represent. They should ask the following questions:

- Why did this happen?
- How might the characters feel?
- What might happen next?
- How important is "X" character?

Author's Use of Language

Author's Purpose

Expository texts typically share information about a given topic. **Persuasive texts** aim to convince readers to think or act a certain way, and *procedural texts* generally give step-by-step or "how-to" instructions in a given discipline. **Nonfiction narratives** tell a true story, perhaps to inspire, educate, bring awareness to a subject, or simply chronicle an important historical event. In order for students to become independent readers and draw their own conclusions about what they read, it is critical that they learn to discern the **author's purpose**.

One obvious approach to teaching children how to reveal an author's purpose is to simply ask children why they think the author wrote this information. These types of open-ended class discussions allow children to express their ideas, explore theories, and consider what others have to say on the subject. Educators can record various answers and then ask the children to return to the text as detectives, looking for clues that support each theory.

Another approach to uncovering the author's purpose is for students to take a closer look at the written structure of the text and the vocabulary usage. For example, is the text's structure written in chronological order, simply listing events as they occurred? Does the text open up with a problem that is then resolved? Is the author using cause/effect or compare/contrast vocabulary? Learning about the structure of the text gives great insight into the author's purpose.

When children develop reading fluency, they are able to read a text with minimal to no errors, with consistent speed, and with appropriate expression, and they learn to connect with what they are reading on a personal level. As children read through an informational text, educators may ask how the students are feeling. Did they begin feeling one way and end up feeling another by the end of the text? When children examine their own personal feelings with regard to what they have read, they will be in a better position to explore the author's purpose.

Once children have had several opportunities to explore the author's purpose using a variety of informational texts, prompting them to write their own informational texts will help them to develop and strengthen a better understanding about writing with a purpose. Perhaps they can write a procedural text that lists the steps in how to ride a bike, or they can write a persuasive paper to try to convince their teacher that extra free time during the school day stimulates learning.

Learning to identify an author's purpose connects children with their reading on a deeper level. Instead of believing everything they read, they will begin to understand that there are many reasons why authors write, and they will further understand that they possess the ability to draw their own conclusions and make their own decisions on any given topic.

Types, Structures, and Features of Informational Texts

Text Features and Organizational Patterns

Informational text is specifically designed to relate factual information, and although it is open to a reader's interpretation and application of the facts, the structure of the presentation is carefully designed to lead the reader to a particular conclusion or central idea. When reading informational text, it is important that readers are able to understand its organizational structure as the structure often directly relates to an author's intent to inform and/or persuade the reader.

The first step in identifying the text's structure is to determine the thesis or main idea. The thesis statement and organization of a work are closely intertwined. A **thesis statement** indicates the writer's purpose and may include the scope and direction of the text. It may be presented at the beginning of a text or at the end, and it may be explicit or implicit.

Once a reader has a grasp of the thesis or main idea of the text, he or she can better determine its organizational structure. Test takers are advised to read informational text passages more than once in order to comprehend the material fully. It is also helpful to examine any text features present in the text including the table of contents, index, glossary, headings, footnotes, and visuals. The analysis of these features and the information presented within them, can offer additional clues about the central idea and structure of a text. The following questions should be asked when considering structure:

- How does the author assemble the parts to make an effective whole argument?
- Is the passage linear in nature and if so, what is the timeline or thread of logic?
- What is the presented order of events, facts, or arguments? Are these effective in contributing to the author's thesis?

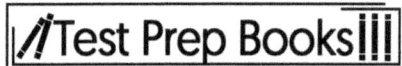

- How can the passage be divided into sections? How are they related to each other and to the main idea or thesis?

- What key terms are used to indicate the organization?

Next, test takers should skim the passage, noting the first line or two of each body paragraph—the *topic sentences*—and the conclusion. Key **transitional terms**, such as *on the other hand, also, because, however, therefore, most importantly*, and *first*, within the text can also signal organizational structure. Based on these clues, readers should then be able to identify what type of organizational structure is being used. The following organizational structures are most common:

- **Problem/solution**—organized by an analysis/overview of a problem, followed by potential solution(s)

- **Cause/effect**—organized by the effects resulting from a cause or the cause(s) of a particular effect

- **Spatial order**—organized by points that suggest location or direction—e.g., top to bottom, right to left, outside to inside

- **Chronological/sequence order**—organized by points presented to indicate a passage of time or through purposeful steps/stages

- **Comparison/Contrast**—organized by points that indicate similarities and/or differences between two things or concepts

- **Order of importance**—organized by priority of points, often most significant to least significant or vice versa

Informational Text Structures
- **Biography:** This is a text that shares intimate details of someone's life. Specifically, this is when an author writes such a text about someone else. If the author were to write about himself or herself, it would be called an **autobiography**.

- **How-to**: This is a text that details step-by-step instructions on how to achieve a specific outcome. This could range anywhere from a recipe to an automobile manual.

- **Description**: This kind of writing is typically in the context a product. A list of characteristics, features, or ingredients may be included in this type of text.

- **Cause and Effect**: This type of writing is used to highlight a relationship between two or more things. It is often used in bringing attention to the origins and endings of something or an event.

- **Sequence**: This writing is used to give a chronological account of events that have or that will take place.

Organization of a Text

There are five basic elements inherent in effective writing, and each will be discussed throughout the various subheadings of this section.

- **Main idea**: The driving message of the writing, clearly stated or implied

- **Clear organization**: The effective and purposeful arrangement of the content to support the main idea

- **Supporting details/evidence**: Content that gives appropriate depth and weight to the main idea of the story, argument, or information

- **Diction/tone**: The type of language, vocabulary, and word choice used to express the main idea, purposefully aligned to the audience and purpose

- **Adherence to conventions of English**: Correct spelling, grammar, punctuation, and sentence structure, allowing for clear communication of ideas

Consider this graphic:

Using Technology to Support Students

Critically Examine Online Resources and Foster Digital Literacy

Using Technology to Conduct Final Research Products

Teachers are learning to adapt their writing instruction to integrate today's technology standards and to enhance engagement in the writing process. The key is to still build a strong foundation of the fundamentals of writing while using current technology. Gone are the days when writing relied solely on handwritten pieces and when the tools of the trade were pencils, paper, hardback dictionaries, and encyclopedias. Online resources are now the backbone of the writing experience. It is now possible to integrate photo, video, and other interactive components into a completed project to provide a well-

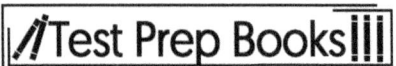

rounded engagement with media. In order to have an education conducive to college and career readiness and success, students need online research and digital media writing skills.

There are many compelling reasons to teach students to be digitally aware and prudent users of technology when it comes to their writing. With current digital technology, the writing process has become a much more collaborative experience. In higher education and in career settings, collaborative skills are essential. Publishing and presenting are now simplified such that completed work is often read by a wide variety of audiences. Writing can be instantly shared with parents, peers, educators, and the general public, including experts in the field. Students are more apt to take an interest in the writing process when they know that others are reading their writing. Feedback is also simplified because so many platforms allow comments from readers. Teachers can be interactive with the students throughout the process, allowing formative assessment and integration of personalized instruction. Technology is simply a new vehicle for human connection and interactivity.

Reference Materials and Media Resources

A student may be exposed to a plethora of technology, but this does not mean that she or he necessarily knows how to use it for learning. The teacher is still responsible for guiding, monitoring, and scaffolding the students toward learning objectives. It is critical that educators teach students how to locate credible information and to reliably cite their sources using bibliographies. Platforms and apps for online learning are varied and plentiful. Here are some ideas for how to use technology for writing instruction in the classroom:

- Use a projector with a tablet to display notes and classwork for the group to see. This increases instructional time because notes are already available rather than having to be written in real-time. This also provides the ability to save, email, and post classwork and notes for students and parents to access on their own time. A student can work at their own pace and still keep up with instruction. Student screens can be displayed for peer-led teaching and sharing of class work.

- More technology in class means less paperwork. Digital drop-boxes can be used for students to turn in assignments. Teachers can save paper, keep track of student revisions of work, and give feedback electronically.

- Digital media can be used to differentiate instruction for multiple learning styles and multiple skill levels. Instead of using standardized textbook learning for everyone, teachers can create and collect resources for individualizing course content.

- Inquiry- and problem-based learning is easier with increased collaborative capabilities provided by digital tools.

- Digital textbooks and e-readers can replace hardback versions of text that are prone to damage and loss. Students can instantly access definitions for new words, as well as annotate and highlight useful information without ruining a hardbound book.

- Library databases can be used to locate reliable research information and resources. There are digital tools for tracking citation information, allowing annotations for internet content, and for storing internet content.

- Mobile devices may be used in the classroom to encourage reading and writing when students use them to text, post, blog, and tweet.

Comprehension of Literary and Informational Text

- PowerPoint and other presentation software can be used to model writing for students and to provide a platform for presenting their work.

- Students can create a classroom blog, review various blog sites, and use blogs as they would diaries or journals. They can even write from the perspective of the character in a book or a famous historical person.

- Web quests can be used to help guide students on research projects. They can get relevant information on specific topics and decide what pieces to include in their writing.

- Students can write about technology as a topic. They can "teach" someone how to use various forms of technology, specific learning platforms, or apps.

- Students can create webpages, make a class webpage, and then use it to help with home-school communication.

- Online feedback and grading systems can be used. There are many to choose from. This may allow students to see the grading rubric and ask questions or receive suggestions from the teacher.

- Students and teachers can use email to exchange ideas with other schools or experts on certain topics that are being studied in the classroom.

- Game show-style reviews can be created for units of study to use on computers or on an overhead projector.

- A wiki website can be created that allows students to collaborate, expand on each other's work, and do peer editing and revision.

- Publishing tools can be used to publish student work on the web or in class newspapers or social media sites.

Personalize Learning Experiences for Students of Different Needs

Instructors retrieve data from both informal and formal assessments. This data, whether written or gained through observation, is highly valuable in determining the effectiveness of teaching methods. Data-driven instruction guides reading improvement for all students simply because the data provides clear indications of where students are facing reading challenges or demonstrating strengths.

Differentiated instruction acknowledges that, while a group of students may be learning the same subject, the way each student learns and processes the subject is different. Differentiation involves looking at the different learning methods and reading areas and identifying which ones students respond to. Educators can then tailor, or differentiate, lessons to build on these skills and expedite the learning process. Differentiated instruction is divided into **interest-based** and **ability-based** instruction.

Much of a student's performance is based on their interest in the subject at hand. Sometimes a student may show difficulty reading because he or she is not engaged in the material. One way to encourage reading growth is to allow students to choose their learning activities. This will give students ownership over their own education, enabling them to have fun and to use specific activities that help them improve their reading abilities. For example, students more interested in visual activities may find reading more beneficial than listening to oral reading exercises.

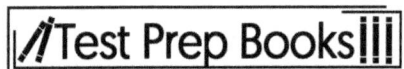

Comprehension of Literary and Informational Text

Ability-based differentiation focuses on three core areas that determine reading proficiency and build skill. The first area of focus examines students' conceptual understanding of reading. If a teacher uses vocabulary or reading comprehension exercises in class, they will be able to examine how students are performing and modify instruction to address any confusion. This can also indicate students' preferences as well. The second differentiation looks at how students analyze and use the reading. Instructors must look at how students respond to questions and whether their interpretation is accurate. The final differentiation looks at how students evaluate and perform reading, creating a reaction that responds to the reading. The third differentiation looks at interpretation with the added step of using this knowledge to write or say something without being prompted. Identifying issues in one of these areas will narrow down where more emphasis must be placed to improve reading skills. Each reading area will affect the other two; improving one differentiated area will impact the others.

Support Active Learning Across Content Areas
Using Technology Tools for Effective Communication

Different technological tools serve different functions. To function in the developing world, students need to learn and understand **digital literacy**—the knowledge, dexterity, and critical thinking skills involved in using technology to create, evaluate, and present information. The best techniques for instructing students on choosing and using technological tools involve educating them on the advantages and disadvantages of each, demonstrating how to use them, breaking down their different aspects, assigning students homework or projects in which they will utilize different technological resources, and instructing them on when it is appropriate to use each kind. The most common types of tools used for communication are as follows:

- Smartphones/apps
- Email
- Microsoft Office
- iMovie
- Skype
- Twitter
- Facebook
- Instagram
- Google Drive
- Various blogging websites
- Online bulletin boards
- Wikis

A good way to introduce students to varying technological tools is by using them in the classroom. It would be helpful to teach students how to use a PowerPoint presentation, for example, by giving a PowerPoint presentation. If a student asks a question to which the teacher does not know the answer, they can discover the answer together by using a reliable source on the Internet, projecting the process on the board, so that they can see exactly how it's done. Students can also receive homework and updates on school and classroom events through a personal blog or class bulletin board the teacher has designed so that they may become familiar with using online communication. Students can also be assigned to use personal blogs to practice and improve their writing skills.

The most effective method for learning new skills is a hands-on approach. Students can be educated on the pros and cons of each technological tool, but the best way for them to learn is to allow them to find out for themselves by assigning projects and asking them to give the reasoning behind choosing a specific tool. For example, they may be asked to do a project on some aspect of the Revolutionary War by choosing a media format. Ideas may include the following:

- Doing a presentation
- Filming and editing a video re-enactment of a great battle
- Writing a script in Microsoft Word or in a Google doc and having classmates act it out
- Creating Facebook statuses from the viewpoints of the forefathers in modern colloquial language
- Having a "Twitter war" between the British and the Colonials
- Asking various people to participate in a collaborative Wiki or Google Doc in which many people give their versions of aspects of the Revolutionary War
- Writing a blog narrating life as a soldier
- Posting photos of the signing of the Declaration of Independence

Students can then give their presentations to the classroom so that students can learn about the topic through different presentation styles.

Another way to engage students in using technology is to have them communicate with each other through the various methods of communication—e.g., starting a class Google Doc, creating a classroom Facebook group, or using a discussion board. This is also an excellent opportunity to encourage students to use Standard English through all methods of communication to enhance their writing skills and instill a sense of professionalism, which they will need throughout their lives.

For example, requiring that all students use complete sentences, proper spelling, and grammar through Facebook, Twitter, or blogs associated with homework or projects will encourage them to do so in their daily lives as well. Another example is requiring that students select tweets from their favorite celebrities or politicians, analyze their meaning and purpose, correct their grammar and spelling, and re-tweet them in the correct way. There are countless ways in which technology can be used in the classroom to enhance students' understanding of digital communication; all it requires is a little creativity.

Evaluating Technology-Based Strategies

It is hard to find a technological tool that will not be useful for students to explore. The more a student engages with the numerous different types of technology, the more digitally literate that student will become. Each type is effective and brings value to the table in its own way. When evaluating the effectiveness of a specific technology-based strategy, it's important to consider how this method is enhancing the student's digital literacy, as well as their critical thinking and communication skills. It is also necessary to evaluate the technology itself by asking relevant questions:

- Is it appropriate for the average age of the students in the classroom?
- Is it user friendly?
- Does it work consistently?
- Are there multiple ways to get help on learning how to use it?

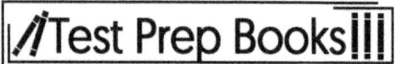

Comprehension of Literary and Informational Text

- Are there trouble-shooting options?
- Does it have good reviews?
- Is it relevant to the content of the curriculum?
- Does it support and align to the learning objective?
- Is it more distracting than it is useful?
- Is it a tool that is/will be used often in the real world?
- Can it be used for more than one project or assignment?

One very effective teaching strategy is **collaborative learning**, in which two or more students work together to develop a project, work through an idea, or solve a problem. This method allows for students to play off each other's strengths and different experiences and learn how to communicate with their classmates to achieve goals. Technology can be used for collaborative learning in Google Drive, Skype, Google Hangouts, Nearpod, Padlet, and Periscope, in creating PowerPoint presentations together, or by conducting surveys with websites like Survey Monkey.

Another effective teaching method is **discussion**, in which students are given a topic or create a topic themselves and then use technology to engage in discourse. This can be done via discussion boards, such as ProBoards or Boardhost, or done live through programs such as Skype or Hangouts. Discussion strategies are extremely effective for enhancing communication skills and digital literacy.

A third method is **active learning**, in which the student engages in activities such as reading, writing, or teaching the subject to another student. Blogging is a great way to encourage active learning as it provides a medium through which students can reflect on what they've learned and respond to comments posted by the teacher or other students. Most of the suggestions made in the previous section—making presentations, creating video re-enactments, writing scripts, having mock Twitter or Facebook comment wars—are all forms of active learning. These types of activities solidify events, ideas, and skills in a student's mind in a way that memorization or flashcards do not as they utilize many different types of thinking and interaction.

One method that a teacher may employ depending on the class and circumstances is **distance learning**. Distance learning is any type of teaching method in which the student and teacher are not in the same place simultaneously. Many professors utilize distance learning through different kinds of technologies, including a live virtual lecture, computer simulations, interactive discussions, and virtual/audio learning environments. These strategies have their advantages in that one teacher can teach a large number of students and multiple locations, and students can communicate with fellow classmates across the globe.

Auditory learning is a strategy in which a student learns through listening. This typically happens via recorded lectures that can be downloaded as podcasts onto a classroom website, discussion board, or some other audio-simulated learning environment. **Visual learning** is learning through watching, in which ideas and concepts are illustrated through images, videos, or by observing a teacher complete a task, explain a concept, or solve a problem. This can be achieved through recorded videos, cartoons, virtual lectures, or by sitting in the classroom. Additionally, **kinesthetic learning** is active learning through physical interaction with an object or actively solving a problem, as opposed to passively listening or watching.

Every student has a different learning style which is unique to them—some learn better through listening while others learn better through doing. The best teaching methods employ all different learning strategies so that all the senses are engaged and every student has a chance at learning material based on their individual learning needs. Technology offers educators the tools do that.

Using Evidence to Support Predictions, Opinions, and Conclusions

Text evidence is the information readers find in a text or passage that supports the main idea or point(s) in a story. In turn, text evidence can help readers draw conclusions about the text or passage. The information should be taken directly from the text or passage and placed in quotation marks. Text evidence provides readers with information to support ideas about the text so that they do not rely simply on their own thoughts. Details should be precise, descriptive, and factual. Statistics are a great piece of text evidence because they provide readers with exact numbers and not just a generalization. For example, instead of saying "Asia has a larger population than Europe," authors could provide detailed information such as, "In Asia there are over 4 billion people, whereas in Europe there are a little over 750 million." More definitive information provides better evidence to readers to help support their conclusions about texts or passages.

Practice Quiz

1. Carson wants to improve his students' metacognition. What would be a good step for him to take?
    I. Asking students why they think what they think
    II. Always telling his students whether their ideas are correct or incorrect
    III. Encouraging students to think about their own learning styles and use study techniques that work for them
    IV. Allowing his students to choose books that interest them

    a. I and II
    b. II and III
    c. I and III
    d. II and IV

2. Why is annotation a beneficial exercise for students?
    a. It teaches them to think independently.
    b. It helps them learn to identify key points.
    c. It teaches them to write faster.
    d. It helps shy students engage in discussion.

3. Which statement about choosing a reading program for learner-centered education is true?
    a. Use older materials because they have been tested by numerous teachers.
    b. Use a program that offers options so that you can tailor the program to your students.
    c. Never blend two programs, as it makes things confusing for the students.
    d. Use the program that the other teachers in your school are using.

4. A class silently reads a passage on the American Revolution. Once they are done, the teacher asks the students to name the two sides who were fighting, the reason they were fighting, and the winner. What skill is the teacher gauging?
    a. Orthographic development
    b. Fluency
    c. Comprehension
    d. Phonics

5. A teacher assigns a writing prompt in order to assess her students' reading skills. Which of the following can be said about this form of reading assessment?
    a. It is the most beneficial way to assess reading comprehension.
    b. It is invalid because a student's ability to read and write are unrelated.
    c. It is erroneous since the strength of a student's reading and writing vocabulary may differ.
    d. It is the worst way to assess reading comprehension.

See answers on next page

Answer Explanations

1. C: Metacognition is the ability to think about one's thoughts. Asking students why they think what they think, option *I*, improves metacognition by compelling students to examine their thoughts. Encouraging students to think about their learning style, option *III*, also hones metacognition. Always correcting or praising students' ideas, option *II*, does not contribute to metacognition because it encourages students to think there is just one right answer. Allowing students to choose their own books, option *IV*, is a way of sparking student engagement, not fostering metacognition.

2. B: Annotating texts teaches students to determine what information is important. Choices *A* and *C* may be true in some cases, but they are not necessarily related to annotation. Choice *D* is false because annotating does not involve class discussion.

3. B: Flexibility is a central component of learner-centered education. Choice *A* is untrue because older materials may rely on outdated research. Choice *C* is false because combining two programs may allow teachers to benefit from the strengths of both methods. While talking to other teachers is a great idea, Choice *D* is not correct because your coworkers are not necessarily using the best programs in their classes.

4. C: Comprehension is the level of content understanding that a student demonstrates after reading. Orthographic development is a cumulative process for learning to read, with each skill building on the previously mastered skill. Fluency is an automatic recognition and accurate interpretation of text. Phonics is the ability to apply letter-sound relationships and letter patterns in order to accurately pronounce written words.

5. C: There are five types of vocabulary: listening, speaking, written, sight, and meaning. Most often, listening vocabulary contains the greatest number of words. This is usually followed by speaking vocabulary, sight reading vocabulary, meaning vocabulary, and written vocabulary. Formal written language usually utilizes a richer vocabulary than everyday oral language. Thus, students show differing strengths in reading vocabulary and writing vocabulary. Likewise, a student's reading ability will most likely differ when assessed via a reading assessment versus a writing sample.

Writing

Written Expression

Writing as a Recursive Process that Supports Self-Evaluation and Expression

Like with any complicated processes, writing development begins with the simplest form of indiscernible scribbles and progresses to fully formed words and, finally, to clearly written sentences and paragraphs. This is actually a complicated cognitive process that takes time and instruction to improve.

With very young students, emphasis can focus on simply making letters clear. After all, letters and word formation are the starting blocks of written language. The next phase in development can focus on actually creating words and making sure they are spelled correctly. When students are at the sentence development stage, grammar and linguistic rules become a priority. The foundations of the English language need to be firm in order for students to have good writing. When students have progressed to more advanced levels and are composing fully formed sentences with a specific purpose, it's time to incorporate content-related feedback.

Feedback at all levels of writing development is crucial; this is how students will learn to correct mistakes and strengthen growing skills. Instructor feedback must be clear while also being sensitive to the students' struggles or backgrounds. Differentiated instruction may be required to bolster students' writing skills. A good starting point for overall writing instruction is to introduce students to the stages of writing an original piece.

The goal with the stages of writing is to build on the previous work. The prewriting stage is the time for students to just write down ideas and plan on how they will approach the topic at hand. The actual writing stage then dovetails on this fluidly because the student already has a framework of what the writing will focus on and how they will present information. In addition to practicing physical writing, these stages focus on critical-thinking and planning skills and may lessen the student's stress before they write and receive feedback. Feedback on the initial writing, or first draft, is key. The instructor should be able to assess any difficulties and then steer the student toward improving their writing in the revision stage. After revisions, instructors should examine how effective their feedback was in helping the writing improve overall.

Methods of Feedback in the Writing Process

It is almost as important to provide feedback and evaluate a student's skill level as it is to teach. Most classes utilize both formative and summative assessments as a grading template. Although assessment and grading are not the same thing, assessments are often used to award a grade. A **formative assessment** monitors the student's progress in learning and allows continuous feedback throughout the course in the form of homework and in-class assignments, such as quizzes, writing workshops, conferences, or inquiry-based writing prompts. These assessments typically make up a lower percent of the overall grade. Alternatively, a **summative assessment** compares a student's progress in learning against some sort of standard, such as against the progress of other students or by the number of correct answers. These assessments usually make up a higher percent of the overall grade and come in the form of midterm or final exams, papers, or major projects.

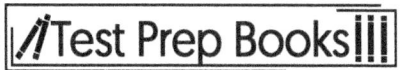

One evidence-based method used to assess a student's progress is a rubric. A **rubric** is an evaluation tool that explicitly states the expectations of the assignment and breaks it down into different components. Each component has a clear description and relationship to the assignment as a whole. For writing, rubrics may be **holistic**, judging the overall quality of the writing, or they can be **analytic**, in which different aspects of the writing are evaluated (e.g., structure, style, word choices, and punctuation).

Rubrics can be used in all aspects of a curriculum, including reading comprehension, oral presentations, speeches, performances, papers, projects, and listening comprehension. They are usually formative in nature but can be summative depending on the purpose. Rubrics allow instructors to provide specific feedback and allow students to understand the expectations for an assignment.

An example of an analytic rubric is displayed below:

Name _____   Date _____

Essay Rubric	4 Mastery	3 Satisfactory	2 Needs Improvement	1 Poor
Writing Quality	-Excellent usage of voice and style -Outstanding organizational skills -Wealth of relevant information	-Style and voice of essay was interesting -Mostly organized -Useful amount of information	-Inconsistent style and voice -Lacked clear organization -Small amount of useful information	-No noticeable style or voice -Virtually no organization -No relevant information
Grammar Conventions	-Essentially no mistakes in grammar -Correct spelling throughout	-Minor amount of grammar and spelling mistakes	-Many errors in grammar conventions and spelling	-Too many grammatical errors to understand the meaning of the piece

Rubrics and conferencing are both methods that provide useful *feedback*, one of the most important elements in the progress of a student's learning. **Feedback** is essentially corrective instruction delivered in writing, either verbally or non-verbally. Research has shown that the following techniques are the most effective when giving feedback:

Being Specific

For a student to know exactly how he or she is doing, feedback should be directed towards specific components of a student's writing, listening, or speaking skills, not a holistic overview. For example, writing "Excellent!" on a student's paper or homework is not useful information as it's unclear what was done well. A paper should provide useful comments throughout the body of the work, for example, "Wording is confusing here," or "Great use of adjectives." However, instructor comments should not overwhelm the student's writing; they should be used to focus their attention on specific areas of success or improvement. This encourages the student to keep doing what he or she is doing well and work on what needs improvement without being overwhelmed.

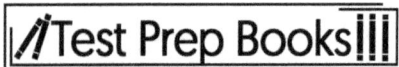

Being Sensitive
Giving feedback is precarious in nature as it entirely depends upon the emotional and mental states of the receiver. Some students do well with "tough love," while others may be discouraged and disheartened to see a slew of comments on their paper. Teachers should pay attention to how a student reacts to feedback. As a general rule, feedback should focus more on the positives so as not to damage self-esteem, while teaching students new techniques for self-correction, instead of simply criticizing what they've done. Also, it's important to try and be aware of the types of feedback each student responds the most effectively to, for example, providing oral feedback for students who don't read well.

Being Prompt
Feedback should be presented sooner rather than later, so that students will not have time to repeat mistakes they are unaware of that may become habitual. Studies have shown that students who are given immediate feedback display a greater increase in performance than those who were given feedback later in the term. As soon as the action has happened, it is important give the appropriate praise or critique so that the student associates the feedback with the action.

Being Explicit
It is important to explain the purpose of the feedback before it is given so that a student does not feel controlled, too closely examined, or competitive. This can cause the learner to feel self-conscious and discourage him or her from performing their best. The importance of feedback and how it is meant to improve on a personal skill set should be explained to the student.

Being Focused
Teachers should try and keep the feedback in alignment with the goal the student is expected to achieve. Too much feedback, especially if it is unrelated to the goal, can be overwhelming and distracting from the purpose of the assignment or paper.

Here are some other tips to consider when giving feedback:

- Teachers should be aware of their body language and facial expressions when giving feedback—a frown or grimace can be very discouraging, even if the written feedback was mostly positive.

- It's conducive to concentrate on one thing at a time. If a student submits a paper with a lot of errors, for example, it may be helpful to identify a prevalent pattern of error and work through strategies to correct it so that student does not feel overwhelmed.

- Using effective rubrics can make all the difference—letting students know exactly what is expected will provide them with a basis on which to model their techniques and skills.

- Students should be educated on giving feedback. This can be demonstrated by example and through instruction how to give feedback in a positive, constructive way and correct any behavior that trends toward disrespect or excessive competition. Students should also provide feedback to the teacher as well.

- Teachers should not give the same comments to every student, but make them personal.

- When offering criticism, teachers should always offer tips for how the student can improve.

- It's important to avoid personal comments, e.g., "You're so smart!" or "Math isn't your best subject." Rather, the comments should focus on the writing: e.g., "The organization of this paper is clear."

- Students shouldn't be compared to each other, e.g., "Look how perfectly Victor composed this sentence!" This can galvanize the students into competing with one another.

High-Quality Writing

High-quality writing takes more than simply good writing skills and a knowledge of vocabulary. High-quality writing takes a lot of planning, writing, and revising in order to meet the standards of the audience. Many factors go into high-quality writing, but some major ones, including content, voice, and word choice, are listed below:

Content

The **content** of a piece of writing includes the ideas, structure, language, and effect of a particular text. Content begins with a writer being able to effectively brainstorm and research their topic in order to obtain credibility as an author. Thorough research of a topic and proper citation is the first step in creating good content. Organization of the text is also important to high-quality content, as is knowledge of vocabulary and sentence structure. Finally, good writing content will have an intended effect on the audience, whether that be persuading the audience to act or informing them of how something is done.

Voice

The voice an author selects is also important to note. An author's **voice** is that element of style that indicates their personality. It's important that authors move us as readers; therefore, they will choose a voice that helps them do that. An author's voice may be satirical or authoritative. It may be light-hearted or serious in tone. It may be silly or humorous as well. Voice, as an element of style, can be vague in nature and difficult to identify, since it's also referred to as an author's tone, but it is that element unique to the author. It is the author's "self." A reader can expect an author's voice to vary across literary genres. A non-fiction author will generally employ a more neutral voice than an author of fiction, but use caution when trying to identify voice. Do not confuse an author's voice with a particular character's voice.

Word Choice

An author's choice of words—also referred to as **diction**—helps to convey their meaning in a particular way. Through diction, an author can convey a particular tone—e.g., a humorous tone, a serious tone—in order to support the thesis in a meaningful way to the reader.

Connotation is when an author chooses words or phrases that invoke ideas or feelings other than their literal meaning. An example of the use of connotation is the word *cheap*, which suggests something is poor in value or negatively describes a person as reluctant to spend money. When something or someone is described this way, the reader is more inclined to have a particular image or feeling about it or him/her. Thus, connotation can be a very effective language tool in creating emotion and swaying opinion. However, connotations are sometimes hard to pin down because varying emotions can be associated with a word. Generally, though, connotative meanings tend to be fairly consistent within a specific cultural group.

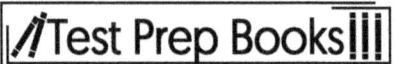

Denotation refers to words or phrases that mean exactly what they say. It is helpful when a writer wants to present hard facts or vocabulary terms with which readers may be unfamiliar. Some examples of denotation are the words *inexpensive* and *frugal*. *Inexpensive* refers to the cost of something, not its value, and *frugal* indicates that a person is conscientiously watching their spending. These terms do not elicit the same emotions that *cheap* does.

Authors sometimes choose to use both, but what they choose and when they use it is what critical readers need to differentiate. One method isn't inherently better than the other; however, one may create a better effect, depending upon an author's intent. If, for example, an author's purpose is to inform, to instruct, and to familiarize readers with a difficult subject, their use of connotation may be helpful. However, it may also undermine credibility and confuse readers. An author who wants to create a credible, scholarly effect in their text would most likely use denotation, which emphasizes literal, factual meaning and examples.

Systematic, Explicit Methods to Teach the Steps of the Writing Process

An introduction to the writing process might begin with a discussion. Teachers can gauge students' knowledge about writing by asking them questions about the writing process, its steps, and its purpose. They may also ask about students' previous experiences with writing. It's important to emphasize that writing is a process, not something students complete once and move on from.

Before expecting students to write, teachers should model each step in the writing process. Based on a chosen topic, the teacher can brainstorm aloud, walking through their thought process and describing different methods for recording the results (for example, in a list, in an outline, or on a concept map). Students would then be given time to brainstorm about their own topics.

Next, the teacher may choose to share samples of drafts from previous students or ones they've completed themselves. Even better, they can model their thought process aloud in front of the class, writing a rough draft while the students watch. **Anchor charts** help to remind students what to include (for example, beginning, middle, and end, and details) and what not to worry about in this step (for example, mistakes, neatness, structure).

The **revision step** includes changes like removing unnecessary information, adding helpful information, and moving text to improve flow. The teacher can point out the issues in the rough draft and make the appropriate edits, incorporating the use of a checklist or anchor chart if one is provided.

In the editing process, the teacher reviews the spelling, grammar, and punctuation of the students' writing. The **editing step** is a great time to catch any errors the students may have missed. This is a good time for a teacher-student conference to review the draft. Peer conferences are also an option. The teacher can act out a peer review conference with one student to show students what is expected from a peer review conference.

Before final submission, the teacher should share the final versions of the papers they've been working on as models, highlighting their strengths in how they meet the parameters of the assignment, especially compared to the rough drafts. Before publishing their final polished draft, students should read over their writing aloud and add necessary details (for example, a title and illustrations). Again, a checklist or anchor chart can be helpful.

Once all writing is complete, students can take turns sharing the final product in small groups or with the class. Peer feedback at this point can help guide future improvements in the next writing assignment.

The easiest way to guide the writing process is to give students time to work on it in class. This allows the teacher to check on students' progress and offer feedback as they go through the writing process. To promote improvement, teachers can make each part of the writing process (for example, rough draft, peer review conference) a part of the final grade for the assignment.

Strategies for Integrating Reading and Writing

Summarizing

Teaching students to summarize is another comprehension and analysis technique. They can complete rewriting exercises here as well. Students just need to do three things when they employ this technique. They should recall what they read, identify the main point of the texts, and exclude unnecessary information. Summarizing does not have to take place after students have finished reading texts; they can do it as they go along. Eventually, this type of summarizing will be second nature, and students will be able to assess the texts without stopping.

Teach students to summarize information. For example, you could ask students to take notes on the most important points in a text and then write a summary. Younger students do better with simple oral summaries, while older students can handle more complicated written work. Summarizing is a great way to improve comprehension. It also tests analysis skills, as students need to discern which points are important and which are just details.

Annotation

Teach your students to annotate texts by highlighting and making notes in the margins. For example, you might have students read a confusing passage, then annotate it by highlighting the most important pieces of information and defining difficult words. By annotating texts, students learn to recognize central points and research words or background information that they do not understand.

Teach your students to take notes. For students who are just learning to take notes, it may be helpful to practice reading a text as a class and making notes on the board. Teach your students useful skills like summarizing, picking out main points, and outlining arguments. For example, you could read a passage aloud and ask all the students to take notes. You could then have the class compare notes and write a collaborative summary of the text.

Have students apply metacognition to their comprehension by identifying the elements of a text that they cannot understand. For example, if a student says, "I don't understand this book," ask them to think about the specific aspects that confuse them and build a more detailed phrase like "I don't understand what happens in chapter four," or "I can't understand this word."

Digital Tools

Digital tools are an invaluable resource for the classroom. They can enhance the learning experience by providing new forms of engagement. This benefits both students and teachers. Apps, videos, websites, and games are just a few examples of digital tools that can provide unique educational content. These tools can help students work on collaboration and creativity. Digital tools can also improve accessibility in the classroom. Educational videos can aid visual learners, audiobooks can provide auditory learners with a new reading experience, and kinesthetic learners may learn new skills from building games. These are just a few examples of how digital tools may benefit different types of students.

When implementing digital tools, student engagement often times sees great improvement. Maintaining student interest is a major key to effective learning. Teachers also benefit from digital tools in the learning space. They can record lectures for at-home learning, ease workloads by automating repetitive tasks such as grading, and streamline communication with students and their families. Overall, both students and teachers may benefit from the implementation of digital tools in the classroom. Technology is always advancing, and it is wise to take advantage of the benefits it offers.

Communication

One of the most important elements of a successful classroom is communication. **Communication** is fundamental to creating an environment where students feel welcome and ready to learn. When teachers and students establish solid communication, students will feel more comfortable asking questions, advocating for themselves, and working with others. These are a few ways to improve academic success overall. Communication happens with an active, dedicated approach. This applies to both verbal and non-verbal communication. To enhance verbal communication, teachers may provide positive affirmations when students perform well. A non-verbal communication tip is to face individual students as they speak and maintain comfortable eye contact with them.

Writing

One of the fundamental parts of learning to write well is having your work reviewed. There are many online platforms where students can practice their writing skills and submit it for feedback. This includes both fiction and non-fiction writing. Hemingway Editor is a free website and app that will point out common errors in writing: spelling, grammar, run-on sentences, and confusing wording. If a student is interested in getting feedback from other writers, Scribophile is an online workshop where students can submit their work for critique. This is useful for writers of all skill levels.

Collaboration

There is a plethora of online platforms that encourage collaboration in the classroom. They allow students to share what they are learning with one another, work on group projects, and communicate virtually. Some platforms are utilitarian; others are designed for fun. A utilitarian option is Google Drive, which allows students to share documents, presentations, and more. A fun option is Kahoot, which students can use to create quiz games that an entire class can participate in. This kind of collaborative creation is one way to get students to practice their teamwork.

Publishing

Teachers can also evaluate texts by researching the publisher. Some presses have a record of publishing excellent teaching material; for example, Macmillan/McGraw-Hill and Scholastic both publish high-quality books that are often used in classrooms. Browsing the websites of these and other respected publishers can help you locate good reading material.

It is important that students become familiar with different publishers. Having students research different online publications while doing their work allows them to become familiar with how to identify scholarly information online. They will learn how to read and cite from different kinds of publications. Students can see what goes into publication, and it may encourage them to publish their own writing.

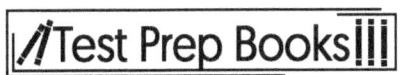

Characteristics and Appropriate Instructional Methods for Teaching the Various Types of Writing

It is important to use appropriate instructional methods for teaching the various types of writing. Although general writing tips can be helpful, different writing types require different instructional methods. The types of writing could be categorized as expository, persuasive, narrative, and descriptive. Expository writing is meant to inform the reader about a concept. In this case, you would want to teach about the use of evidence in writing. Persuasive writing is meant to convince the reader of an argument. In this case, you could want to teach about how to present an opinion in writing. Narrative writing tells a story. In this case, you would want to teach about characters and plot. Descriptive writing presents the setting; it can also present imagery. In this case, you would want to teach about how to engage readers with metaphors and similes. These are just a few examples of how writing types differ and how instruction should vary accordingly.

Informational/Expository

Expository or **informational writing** presents facts and information. Academic essays are one example of this type of writing. To remember the name of this writing type, think of the root connection between the words *expository* and *expose*: the goal of expository writing is to expose the facts about a particular topic. Due to its logical purpose, expository writing should be clear and linear. Writers should use strong evidence to back up their claims. Sources used should be scholarly and unbiased. However, just because expository writing is factual, it does not have to be boring. It is important to keep the writing engaging in order to capture readers' interest.

Argument/Persuasive/Opinion

Persuasive writing is used to convince readers of a particular opinion; it writing should be informative and evidence-based. However, unlike expository writing, it also aims to sway readers to believe in a particular position. One example of persuasive writing would be an article on climate change that also presents a solution that the writer wants readers to support. This type of writing should have a strong thesis statement that lets readers know what the main idea is. It may also be important that the writing read as if it were speaking directly to the reader. This is one effective way to draw the reader in to what the author is saying.

Narrative

The goal of **narrative writing** is to tell a story, whether fictional or not. An example of fictional narrative writing would be a novel; autobiography is nonfictional narrative writing. Narrative writing is often the most personal and creative form of writing. There are multiple types of narrative writing, such as linear, non-linear, viewpoint, and descriptive. Narrative writing may include characters, plot, and setting. These elements help the writer to make the story imaginative and unique. Although narrative writing comes with a high degree of writer freedom, effective narrative writing requires just as much skill and practice as the other types of writing.

Spelling and Grammar

Methods to Connect the Teaching of Decoding and Encoding as Reciprocal Skills

Teaching of decoding and encoding should begin with linking sounds to letters and eventually combinations of letters. To decode a word, students must attribute sounds to letters and blend them together. To spell a word, they must break the word they've heard into individual sounds, remember the letter(s) and patterns that make those sounds, and write them down, which is much more challenging. Simultaneous explicit and systematic instruction in decoding and encoding positively affects students' abilities to read, write, and spell.

Teacher-led practice involves the teacher clearly articulating a sound (phoneme) before having students say the sound and then write the letter(s) that correspond with the sound. Once these skills have been solidified, students can begin segmenting the words they hear, identifying the phonemes, and writing the letter(s) that represent them. First, teachers teach explicitly through modeling, and then they walk students through active, guided practice before having students practice independently. Make practice engaging and multimodal (for example, by incorporating hand gestures and manipulable items).

Instruction should be systematic, starting with simple information and using lessons that sequentially build upon one another toward increasingly complex ideas. The curriculum should outline the progression of teaching letter combination patterns (phonemic awareness) and how they are used in reading and spelling rules. This incremental approach promotes mastery in one topic or skill before moving on to new topics and skills.

Approaches to Spelling Development

Spelling development systematically occurs in stages. Through each of these stages, multisensory strategies can be explicitly taught to help enhance a child's spelling development. Here are the spelling development stages as well as different strategies to help development in each of those stages:

- **Pre-phonetic stage:** This stage begins an individual's spelling development, inclusive of key indicators such an incomplete understanding of the alphabetic principle and letter-sound correspondences. Students in this stage participate in **precommunicative writing**, characterized by the jumbling of abstract letter forms rather than a cohesive group of recognizable letters. These writing samples can be used as informal assessments to monitor students' understanding of the alphabetic principle and of letter-sound correspondences.

- **Semiphonetic stage:** In this stage, students have an understanding that letters denote specific sounds. Though this understanding is there, the student may continue to struggle with letter recognition. In the students' writing, they may use individual letters in place of entire words (e.g., *U* for *you*). In other instances, they may omit multiple syllables within a word altogether. Writing in this stage is likely still incomprehensible. To aid in understanding the students' work, teachers can ask students to include drawings to supplement their writing samples.

- **Phonetic stage:** At this point, students will have mastered letter-sound correspondences. Although their physical representation of the letters may be incorrect, phonetic spellers are capable of writing each letter of the alphabet. Due to their limited sight vocabulary, their spelling may be incorrect; however, these incorrectly spelled words are likely still phonetically accurate. Additionally, students are likely to use one letter to represent a digraph or letter blend (e.g., *f* for /ph/). Spelling instruction of common consonant patterns, short vowel sounds, and common affixes or rimes can begin during the phonetic stage. Word walls are beneficial during this stage as they provide visual groupings of words that share common consonant-vowel patterns or letter clusters. Students should be encouraged to contribute words to the wall. As a result, word walls promote strategic spelling, vocabulary development, common letter combinations, and common morphological units.

- **Transitional stage:** In this stage, the student is growing in their sight vocabulary and has a sustainable understanding of letter-sound correspondences. As a result, their spelling dependence on phonology decreases and instead, their dependence on visual representation and word structure increases. Additionally, students increase in their accuracy of spelling irregular words. During this stage, instructors should differentiate spelling instruction. It is necessary that instruction be guided by data collected through informal observations and assessments so that lessons can be personalized, especially in the areas of sight word recognition, morphology, etymology, reading, and writing. In this stage, students are also ready to begin learning about **homophones**; these are words that sound the same but have different spellings and meanings (e.g., *their* and *there*). Additionally, students should begin practicing writing full sentences. Writing reinforces phonics, vocabulary, and correct spelling of words.

- **Conventional stage:** By this stage, students are comfortable with the basic rules of phonics. They can work with consonants, multiple vowel-consonant blends, homophones, digraphs, and irregular spellings. They should be able to recognize incorrectly spelled words. It is at the conventional stage that spelling instruction can begin to focus on content-specific vocabulary words and words with unusual spellings. Students should practice this content-specific language across a variety of activities and subjects when relevant. Students can keep track of words that they consistently spell incorrectly or find confusing in word banks so they can isolate and eventually eliminate their individualized errors.

Teaching the Structure of Written Language

Rules of Grammar and Mechanics

Before educators teach reading or writing, they should themselves be masters of the language. They should know the conventions of grammar, punctuation, spelling, and structure of language in order to communicate clearly. They must also be able to interpret what students are saying to either affirm or revise it. Teachers are responsible for differentiating instruction so that students at all levels and aptitudes can succeed with language learning. Teachers need to be able to isolate gaps in skill sets and decide which skills need intervention in the classroom.

Teachers are evaluators. They are responsible for making key decisions about a student's educational trajectory based on their assessment of the student's capabilities.

Teachers also have great impact on how students view themselves as learners. Teachers are models. They must be superb examples of educated individuals. Just like with any other subject, people need a strong grasp of the basics of language. They will not be able to learn these things unless the teachers themselves have mastered it.

Teachers foster socialization; socialization to cultural norms and to the everyday practices of the community in which they live is of utmost importance to students' lives. These processes begin at home but continue early in a child's life at school. Teachers play a key role in guiding and scaffolding students' socialization skills. If teachers are to excel in this role, they need to be adept with the use of the English language.

Teachers need to have mastery of the conventions of English including:

- Nouns
- Collective Nouns

- Compound Subjects
- Pronouns
- Subjects, Objects, and Compounds
- Pronoun/Noun Agreement
- Indefinite Pronouns
- Choosing Pronouns
- Adjectives
- Compound Adjectives
- Verbs
- Infinitives
- Verb Tenses
- Participles
- Subject/Verb Agreement
- Active/Passive Voice
- Adverbs
- Double Negatives
- Comparisons
- Double Comparisons
- Prepositions
- Prepositional Phrases
- Conjunctions
- Interjections
- Articles
- Types of sentences
- Subjects and Predicates
- Clauses and Phrases
- Pronoun Reference Problems
- Misplaced Modifiers
- Dangling Participial Phrases
- Punctuation
- Periods
- Commas
- Semicolons and Colons
- Parentheses and Dashes
- Quotation Marks
- Apostrophes
- Hyphens
- Question Marks
- Exclamation Points
- Capitalization
- Spelling
- Noun Plurals
- Prefixes and Suffixes
- Spelling Hurdles
- Abbreviations

Writing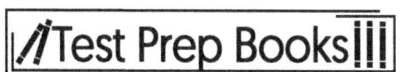

- Pronunciation
- Homonyms and other easy mix-ups

Effective Composing

Good writing is composed of several key elements: development, focus, clarity and coherence, grammatical proficiency, and originality. Different institutions and individual instructors will list such qualities differently, but good composition will have these basic qualities.

Strong compositions have well-developed ideas that are explained clearly throughout the piece. Good writing seems to have been planned and executed without any gaps or confusion. Through their writing, students must essentially develop an idea and line of reasoning that leave readers clear about the focus of the piece. This also means that paragraphs must be arranged in a way that they enhance and expand on the central focus of the paper, using evidence sensibly.

A **writer's focus** is the central point. A successful composition will not only contain a clear focus but carry the focus throughout the piece. The reader should never lose the focus or be confused by it. The way in which the content is presented throughout the text, while remaining focused on the central idea, is key. This is done by the tactical use of evidence surrounding and supporting claims relating to the central idea.

Language can be elegant and creative, but it must be used in a way the reader can understand. Much of a writer's success will depend on the coherence of the written piece. Paragraphs and the ideas within them should not be random but connect together, seamlessly blending into the next section to advance the focus of the writing. Each paragraph should strengthen the claim. Unnecessary paragraphs disrupt the flow of the writing and distract the reader, ultimately weakening the piece. Naturally, the writing should also be grammatically correct and proofed for accurate spelling and sentence structure.

Originality is the defining aspect of a well-written piece. Students should not parrot the writing style or ideas of others but instead write something that is unique. Ideas, and the way they are presented, should be fresh and approach topics in a way that offers a new perspective to the reader.

Effective Written Expression

Written expression refers to the ability of the writer to fluidly communicate meaning and purpose throughout the composition. Essentially, this refers not only to how clear the central focus of the piece is but how well the ideas surrounding the central focus are presented. If the writer can't successfully express the meaning and implications of the idea, the writing will not be strong.

Effective written expression utilizes detailed, clear communication. A writer doesn't need to unload elaborate diction throughout the paragraphs. Such an embellishment can be distracting to the reader, which actually defeats the principles behind effective writing. Sentences should be direct and emphasize language that, while engaging, remains simple enough for the audience to understand. This doesn't mean abstaining from using advanced words but rather keeping sentences direct and to the point. Students should avoid rambling line after line. Avoiding exaggerating language or overdramatic phrasing is also important. Not only can this confuse the reader, it can also harm the reader's credibility.

A simple formula for effective writing is to introduce an idea, discuss it, and then make a conclusion. This applies for the written piece as a whole but must also be used within individual paragraphs. If a writer just introduces idea after idea with no substance, the reader is left with unsubstantiated claims. Without supporting evidence to understand the view, the reader is left with only opinion. With the implementation of facts and supporting details, this opinion is strengthened. Thus, the reasoning behind the central idea is clearly executed and can be considered seriously. This helps the writer achieve credibility.

Paragraph coherence is vital for effective written expression. Paragraph sequencing and information placement are essential to streamlining the entire piece. Evidence and supporting information should be used to transition from one section to another, up to the conclusion. This enables the information to be clearly expressed. The author should strive to write in a way that, as the piece progresses, the focus becomes clearer and more convincing. By the conclusion of the written piece, the author should also restate their thesis to solidify their views and reasoning.

Practice Quiz

Assignment

Use the information in the scenario below to write a reply in which you use your understanding of literacy assessment and instructional strategies to examine this case study. Your response should completely address the following in 400-600 words:

1. Identify a need the student has that may indicate a learning disorder.

2. Describe an effective instructional strategy that would address the need of the student related to the identified learning disorder.

3. Describe some teaching strategies that can be used to help the student improve.

4. Explain why each of your instructional strategies would be effective in helping the student's needs related to reading standards as described in the TEKS for ELAR.

Scenario
Scenario: The following case study is focused on Caleb, a second-grade student.

Caleb's primary instructor has noticed that when Caleb reads material aloud in class, he will often take long pauses and read the sentences slower than the other students. This sometimes causes him to stutter or hesitate during longer sentences. Another issue is that sometimes he will switch the order of the words he sees, for example, putting the word *the* after the word *cat* in a sentence. Despite this, Caleb is very bright and seems to fully grasp the context of the material. He also appears to be engaged when answering questions but is hesitant when having to read in front of the class.

Caleb's teacher has requested that Mr. Breiner, the reading specialist, evaluate Caleb to understand what might be causing his issues. While Caleb is highly intelligent, the teacher is wondering whether his problems with reading may indicate a reading disorder. Mr. Breiner has been requested to present ideas on how to help Caleb's reading skills improve. The teacher wants to be able to learn how to address reading issues like Caleb's in the future, or at least be able to identify core literary issues very early in the developmental stage.

Teacher Notes
1. When reading the sentence, "The next-door neighbors adopted the cat that had been homeless," Caleb switched *the* and *cat*. He also seemed to take longer to sound out *homeless*.

2. Longer sentences seem to cause Caleb confusion when reading aloud.

3. In some of his writing responses, Caleb will sometimes switch the letters within the words or the words themselves.

4. Caleb understands material clearly and gives insightful thoughts aloud. No speech problems were observed.

Assessment and Instructional Decision Making (Constructed Response)

When preparing for the constructed response section of the test, it is important to identify what the scenario is asking you to analyze and to make sure that your ideas are organized. Typically, a constructed response question will give you a scenario to analyze. The scenario will pertain to the science of teaching reading. Additionally, the question will include the information it wants you to specifically address in your response, as well as some additional information that could assist you in constructing your response. When writing for this portion of the test, you should keep in mind what qualifies as effective composition and effective written expression. Planning and organizing your ideas before writing your response, along with understanding what makes for *good* writing, will help you to succeed in this section.

On the test, you may be asked to construct a response based on the follow concepts:

- **Developing Emergent Literacy Learners**
    - Phonological and Phonemic Awareness
    - Phonics
    - Decoding/Encoding
- **Supporting Independent Literacy Learners**
    - Fluency
    - Vocabulary
    - Comprehension
    - Writing
- Responding to Diverse Learners
    - Gifted
    - English Learners
    - Struggling Reads and Writers
    - Students with Learning Disabilities

When constructing a response, you will want to make sure you are following tips for effective expression and composition.

Practice Test

1. In the word *shut*, the *sh* is an example of what?
    a. Consonant digraph
    b. Sound segmentation
    c. Vowel digraph
    d. Rime

2. When students identify the phonemes in spoken words, they are practicing which of the following?
    a. Sound blending
    b. Substitution
    c. Rhyming
    d. Segmentation

3. What is the alphabetic principle?
    a. The understanding that letters represent sounds in words
    b. The ability to combine letters to correctly spell words
    c. The proper use of punctuation within writing
    d. The memorization of all the letters in the alphabet

4. Print awareness includes all EXCEPT which of the following concepts?
    a. The differentiation of uppercase and lowercase letters
    b. The identification of word boundaries
    c. The proper tracking of words
    d. The spelling of sight words

5. When teachers point to words during shared readings, what are they modeling?
    I. Word boundaries
    II. Directionality
    III. One-to-one correspondence
    a. I and II
    b. I and III
    c. II and III
    d. I, II, and III

6. Structural analysis would be the most appropriate strategy in determining the meaning of which of the following words?
    a. Extra
    b. Improbable
    c. Likely
    d. Wonder

7. A student spells *eagle* as *EGL*. This student is performing at which stage of spelling?
    a. Conventional
    b. Phonetic
    c. Semiphonetic
    d. Transitional

8. Spelling instruction should include which of the following?
   I. Word walls
      II. Daily reading opportunities
      III. Daily writing opportunities
      IV. Weekly spelling inventories with words students have studied during the week
   a. I and IV
   b. I, II, and III
   c. I, II, and IV
   d. I, II, III, and IV

9. A kindergarten student is having difficulty distinguishing the letters *b* and *d*. The teacher should do which of the following?
   a. Have the student use a think-aloud to verbalize the directions of the shapes used when writing each letter.
   b. Have the student identify the letters within grade-appropriate texts.
   c. Have the student write each letter five times.
   d. Have the student write a sentence in which all of the letters start with either *b* or *d*.

10. When differentiating phonics instruction for English-language learners (ELLs), teachers should do which of the following?
    a. Increase the rate of instruction
    b. Begin with the identification of word boundaries
    c. Focus on syllabication
    d. Capitalize on the transfer of relevant skills from the learners' original language(s)

11. Which of the following is the most appropriate assessment of spelling for students who are performing at the pre-phonetic stage?
    a. Sight word drills
    b. Phonemic awareness tests
    c. Writing samples
    d. Concepts about print (CAP) test

12. Phonological awareness is best assessed through which of the following?
    a. Identification of rimes or onsets within words
    b. Identification of letter-sound correspondences
    c. Comprehension of an audio book
    d. Writing samples

13. The identification of morphemes within words occurs during the instruction of what?
    a. Structural analysis
    b. Syllabic analysis
    c. Phonics
    d. The alphabetic principle

14. Which of the following pairs of words are homophones?
    a. Playful and replay
    b. To and too
    c. Was and were
    d. Gloomy and sad

Practice Test

15. Nursery rhymes are used in kindergarten to develop what?
    a. Print awareness
    b. Phoneme recognition
    c. Syllabication
    d. Structural analysis

16. High-frequency words such as *be, the*, and *or* are taught during the instruction of what?
    a. Phonics skills
    b. Sight word recognition
    c. Vocabulary development
    d. Structural analysis

17. To thoroughly assess students' phonics skills, teachers should administer assessments that require students to do which of the following?
    a. Decode in context only
    b. Decode in isolation only
    c. Both A and B
    d. Neither A nor B

18. A student is having difficulty pronouncing a word that she comes across when reading aloud. Which of the following is most likely NOT a reason for the difficulty that the student is experiencing?
    a. Poor word recognition
    b. A lack of content vocabulary
    c. Inadequate background knowledge
    d. Repeated readings

19. Which is the largest contributor to the development of students' written vocabulary?
    a. Reading
    b. Directed reading
    c. Direct teaching
    d. Modeling

20. The study of roots, suffixes, and prefixes is called what?
    a. Listening comprehension
    b. Word consciousness
    c. Word morphology
    d. Textual analysis

21. When children begin to negotiate the sounds that make up words in their language independently, what skill(s) are they demonstrating?
    a. Phonological awareness
    b. Phonemes
    c. Phoneme substitution
    d. Blending skills

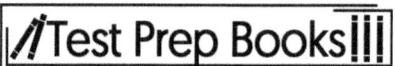

22. What is phonics?
    a. The study of syllabication
    b. The study of onsets and rimes
    c. The study of sound-letter relationships
    d. The study of graphemes

23. Word analysis skills are NOT critical for the development of what area of literacy?
    a. Vocabulary
    b. Reading fluency
    c. Spelling
    d. Articulation

24. What area of study involves mechanics, usage, and sentence formation?
    a. Word analysis
    b. Spelling conventions
    c. Morphemes
    d. Phonics

25. What contributes the most to schema development?
    a. Reading comprehension
    b. Structural analysis
    c. Written language
    d. Background knowledge

26. Which of the following is an essential component of effective reading comprehension?
    a. Reading rate
    b. Genre of text
    c. Size of print
    d. Background knowledge

27. Syntax is best described as what?
    a. The arrangement of words into sentences
    b. The study of language meaning
    c. The study of grammar and language structure
    d. The proper formatting of a written text

28. What do informal reading assessments allow that standardized reading assessments do NOT allow?
    a. The application of grade-level norms toward a student's reading proficiency
    b. The personalization of reading assessments in order to differentiate instruction
    c. The avoidance of partialities in the interpretation of reading assessments
    d. The comparison of an individual's reading performance to that of other students in the class

29. When building a class library, a teacher should be cognizant of the importance of what?
    a. Providing fiction that contains concepts relating to the background knowledge of all students in the class.
    b. Utilizing only nonfiction text that correlates to state and national standards in order to reinforce academic concept knowledge.
    c. Utilizing a single genre of text in order to reduce confusion of written structures.
    d. Including a wide range of fiction and nonfiction texts at multiple reading levels.

Practice Test

30. Samantha is in second grade and struggles with fluency. Which of the following strategies is likely to be most effective in improving Samantha's reading fluency?
   a. The teacher prompts Samantha when she pauses upon coming across an unknown word.
   b. The teacher records Samantha as she reads aloud.
   c. The teacher reads a passage out loud several times to Samantha and then has Samantha read the same passage.
   d. The teacher uses read-alouds and verbalizes contextual strategies that can be used to identify unfamiliar words.

31. Reading fluency is best described as the ability to do what?
   a. Read smoothly and accurately
   b. Comprehend what is read
   c. Demonstrate phonetic awareness
   d. Properly pronounce a list of words

32. Poems are often an effective device when teaching what skill?
   a. Fluency
   b. Spelling
   c. Writing
   d. Word decoding

33. A teacher needs to assess students' accuracy in reading high frequency sight words and irregular sight words that are grade-appropriate. Which of the following strategies would be most appropriate for this purpose?
   a. The teacher gives students a list of words to study for a spelling test that will be administered the following week.
   b. The teacher allows each student to bring their favorite book from home and has each student read their selected text aloud independently.
   c. The teacher administers the Stanford Structural Analysis assessment to determine students' rote memory and application of morphemes contained within the words.
   d. The teacher records how many words each student reads correctly when reading aloud a list of a teacher-selected, grade-appropriate words.

34. What type of texts are considered nonfiction?
   a. Folktales
   b. Memoirs
   c. Fables
   d. Short stories

35. What is a summative assessment?
   a. A formal assessment that is given at the end of a unit of study
   b. An informal assessment that is given at the end of a unit of study
   c. An assessment that is given daily and is usually only a few questions in length, based on the day's objective
   d. An assessment given at the end of the week that is usually based on observation

36. How are typographic features useful when teaching reading comprehension?
    a. Typographic features are graphics used to illustrate the story and help students visualize the text.
    b. Typographic features give the answers in boldfaced print.
    c. Typographic features are not helpful when teaching reading comprehension and should not be used.
    d. Typographic features are print in boldface, italics, and subheadings, used to display changes in topics or to highlight important vocabulary or content.

37. What do English Language Learners need to identify prior to comprehending text?
    a. Vocabulary
    b. Figurative language
    c. Author's purpose
    d. Setting

38. What kind of assessment is most beneficial for students with special needs?
    a. Frequent and ongoing
    b. Weekly
    c. Monthly
    d. Summative assessments only at the end of a unit of study

39. Which is NOT a reason why independent reading is important for developing reading comprehension?
    a. It helps students develop a lifelong love of reading.
    b. It encourages students to read a genre they enjoy.
    c. It provides an opportunity for students to read at their own pace.
    d. It gives students time to visit the reading corner, which is an area of the classroom that is restful and enjoyable.

40. Why are purposeful read-alouds by a teacher important to enhance reading comprehension?
    a. They encourage students to unwind from a long day and reading lesson.
    b. They encourage students to listen for emphasis and tone
    c. They encourage students to compare the author's purpose versus the teacher's objective.
    d. They encourage students to work on important work from earlier in the day while listening to a story.

41. Which of the following is the study of what words mean in certain situations?
    a. Morphology
    b. Pragmatics
    c. Syntax
    d. Semantics

42. What is "text evidence" when referring to answering a comprehension question?
    a. Taking phrases directly from the text itself to answer a question
    b. Using a variety of resources to find the answer
    c. Using technology and websites to locate an answer
    d. Paraphrasing and using a student's own words to answer the question

43. What allows readers to effectively translate print into recognizable speech?
    a. Fluency
    b. Spelling
    c. Phonics
    d. Word decoding

44. Which of the following is the MOST important reason why group-based discussions in the classroom enhance reading comprehension?
    a. They promote student discussions without the teacher present.
    b. They promote student discussions with a friend.
    c. They promote student discussions so that those who didn't understand the text can get answers from another student.
    d. They give all students a voice and allow them to share their answer, rather than one student sharing an answer with the class

45. Which of the following skills is NOT useful when initially helping students understand and comprehend a piece of text?
    a. Graphic organizers
    b. Note-taking
    c. Small intervention groups
    d. Extension projects and papers

46. Why are intervention groups important to advanced learners?
    a. They are not useful, as they do not need intervention in a particular skill.
    b. They can be used to teach struggling students.
    c. They can be given more advanced and complex work.
    d. They can be given tasks to do in the classroom while others are meeting for intervention.

47. Which of the following can be useful when working with intervention groups of struggling readers?
    a. Having the teacher read aloud a text to the students while they take notes
    b. Having students read the text silently
    c. Giving independent work and explaining the directions in detail before they take it back to their seat
    d. Providing games for them to play while the teacher observes

48. What should be taught and mastered first when teaching reading comprehension?
    a. Theme
    b. Word analysis and fluency
    c. Text evidence
    d. Writing

49. What is the method called that teachers use before and after reading to improve critical thinking and comprehension?
    a. Self-monitoring comprehension
    b. KWL charts
    c. Metacognitive skills
    d. Directed reading-thinking activities

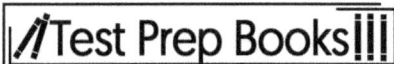

50. When a student looks back at a previous reading section for information, he or she is using which of the following?
    a. Self-monitoring comprehension
    b. KWL charts
    c. Metacognitive skills
    d. Directed reading-thinking activities

51. Which choice of skills is NOT part of Bloom's Taxonomy?
    a. Remembering and understanding
    b. Applying and analyzing
    c. Listening and speaking
    d. Evaluating and creating

52. What is the spelling stage of a student who looks at a word and is able to tell the teacher that the letters spell C-A-T, but who cannot actually say the word?
    a. Alphabetic Spelling
    b. Within Word Pattern Spelling
    c. Derivational Relations Spelling
    d. Emergent Spelling

53. Predicting, summarizing, questioning, and clarifying are steps of what?
    a. Reciprocal teaching
    b. Comprehensive teaching
    c. Activation teaching
    d. Summative teaching

54. What are students utilizing when they ask themselves, What do I know?, What do I want to know?, and What have I learned? and record the answers in a table?
    a. Self-monitoring comprehension
    b. KWL charts
    c. Metacognitive skills
    d. Directed reading-thinking activities

55. What technique might an author use to let the reader know that the main character was in a car crash as a child?
    a. Point of view
    b. Characterization
    c. Figurative language
    d. Flashback

56. A graphic organizer is a method of achieving what?
    a. Integrating knowledge and ideas
    b. Generating questions
    c. Determining point of view
    d. Determining the author's purpose

Practice Test

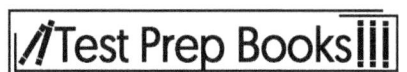

57. A student is trying to decide if a character is telling the truth about having stolen candy. After the student reads that the character is playing with an empty candy wrapper in her pocket, the student decides the character is guilty. This is an example of what?
    a. Flashback
    b. Making inferences
    c. Style
    d. Figurative language

58. What is the method of categorizing text by its structure and literary elements called?
    a. Fiction
    b. Nonfiction
    c. Genre
    d. Plot

59. A reader is distracted from following a story because he is having trouble understanding why a character decided to cut school. He jumps to the next page to find out where the character is headed. This is an example of what?
    a. Self-monitoring comprehension
    b. KWL charts
    c. Metacognitive skills
    d. Directed reading-thinking activities

60. Phonemic awareness, phonics, fluency, vocabulary, and comprehension are the five basic elements of what?
    a. Bloom's Taxonomy
    b. Spelling instruction
    c. Reading education
    d. Genre

61. Which mode of writing aims to inform the reader objectively about a particular subject or idea and typically contains definitions, instructions, or facts within its subject matter?
    a. Argumentative
    b. Informative
    c. Narrative
    d. Descriptive

62. Editorials, letters of recommendation, and cover letters most likely incorporate which writing mode?
    a. Argumentative
    b. Informative
    c. Narrative
    d. Descriptive

63. The type of writing mode an author chooses to use is dependent on which of the following elements?
    a. The audience
    b. The primary purpose
    c. The main idea
    d. Both A and B

64. The rhetorical appeal that elicits an emotional and/or sympathetic response from an audience is known as which of the following?
   a. Logos
   b. Ethos
   c. Pathos
   d. None of the above

65. Which of the following refers to what an author wants to express about a given subject?
   a. Primary purpose
   b. Plot
   c. Main idea
   d. Characterization

66. Which organizational style is used in the following passage?
   There are several reasons why the new student café has not been as successful as expected. One factor is that prices are higher than originally advertised, so many students cannot afford to buy food and beverages there. Also, the café closes rather early; as a result, students go out into town to other late-night gathering places rather than meeting friends at the café on campus.

   a. Cause and effect order
   b. Compare and contrast order
   c. Spatial order
   d. Time order

67. Short, succinct sentences are best written for which of the following audiences?
   a. Adults or people more familiar with a subject
   b. Children or people less familiar a subject
   c. Politicians and academics
   d. University students

68. A student is starting a research assignment on Japanese American internment camps during World War II, but she is unsure of how to gather relevant resources. Which of the following would be the most helpful advice for the student?
   a. Conduct a broad internet search to get a wide view of the subject.
   b. Consult an American history textbook.
   c. Find websites about Japanese culture such as fashion and politics.
   d. Locate texts in the library related to World War II in America and look for references to internment camps in the index.

69. Which of the following should be evaluated to ensure the credibility of a source?
   a. The publisher, the author, and the references
   b. The subject, the title, and the audience
   c. The organization, stylistic choices, and transition words
   d. The length, the tone, and the contributions of multiple authors

70. Which of the following is true of using citations in a research paper?
    a. If a source is cited in the bibliography, it is not necessary to cite it in the paper as well.
    b. In-text citations differ in format from bibliographic citations.
    c. Students should learn one standard method of citing sources.
    d. Books and articles need to be cited, but not websites or multimedia sources.

71. Which of the following is true regarding the integration of source material to maintain the flow of ideas in a research project or paper?
    a. There should be at least one quotation or paraphrase in every paragraph.
    b. If a source is paraphrased instead of being directly quoted, it is not necessary to include a citation.
    c. An author's full name must be used in every signal phrase.
    d. In-text citations should be used to support the paper's argument without overwhelming the student's writing.

72. Which citation style requires the inclusion of the author's last name, the title of the book or article, and its publication date in a bibliography entry?
    a. MLA
    b. APA
    c. Chicago
    d. All of the above

73. Which of the following qualities are necessary for effective speech delivery?
    a. Knowledge, erudite vocabulary, and conviction
    b. Charm, wit, and connection
    c. Confidence, authenticity, and succinctness
    d. Compassion, empathy, and tolerance

74. Which of the following components are advantageous and disadvantageous regarding the use of Microsoft PowerPoint presentations?
    a. They present information that can be taken home and reviewed later, but the audience may choose to read rather than listen.
    b. They allow the audience to follow along with the process of explaining difficult concepts and copy down their own version, but there is limited space that may need to be erased.
    c. They allow for pictures, words, and videos, but they can be distracting from the presence of the speaker.
    d. They allow for participants to interact with the physical world which helps solidify concepts, but they can be distracting if not properly introduced.

75. Which of the following should be considered before utilizing a technological device in the classroom?
    a. The age of the students
    b. Whether it is user friendly
    c. If it will be used in the real world
    d. All of the above

76. Which of the following refers to a teaching strategy in which two or more students work together to develop a project, work through an idea, or solve a problem?
    a. Listening
    b. Collaborative learning
    c. Active learning
    d. Discussion

77. A method of learning in which the student learns through physical interaction with an object is referred to as which of the following?
    a. Auditory Learning
    b. Visual Learning
    c. Kinesthetic Learning
    d. Distance Learning

78. Which of the following defines the stage of writing that involves adding to, removing, rearranging, or re-writing sections of a piece?
    a. The revising stage
    b. The publishing stage
    c. The writing stage
    d. The pre-writing stage

79. A research-proven approach to teaching writing that involves a short lesson, independent writing time, and sharing is known as which of the below?
    a. Writing workshop
    b. Teacher modeling
    c. The writer's notebook
    d. Freewriting

80. Which of the following is true regarding the most effective methods of teaching the writing process?
    a. Instruction should be standardized so that all students should learn writing in the same way.
    b. Feedback should be generalized, giving overall instruction for improvement instead of focusing on certain aspects of writing.
    c. The most important way a student learns is by doing, so they should be given as many opportunities to write as possible.
    d. Students should be compared to one another, so lower-achieving students can model their writing skills on those of more proficient students.

81. Which of the following is true of assessing student writing?
    a. Students should only be given positive feedback so as not to make them feel discouraged.
    b. Students should engage in peer assessments without instructor interference, to increase independent writing skills.
    c. Writing assessments should always be holistic so students get the "big picture" of effective writing.
    d. Writing assessments should be returned in a timely manner.

Practice Test

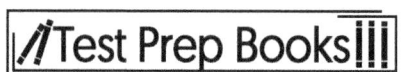

82. Which of the following is an evaluation tool that explicitly states the expectations of an assignment and breaks it down into components and evaluation criteria?
    a. A one-on-one conference
    b. An analytic rubric
    c. A verbal feedback session
    d. A discussion with peers

83. When it comes to class discussions, setting guidelines for the discussion, preventing distracting tangents, and refraining from arguing with students are examples of which of the following?
    a. Cultivating an environment of inclusion and mutual respect
    b. Keeping discussions productive
    c. Encouraging participation
    d. Ensuring accountability

84. If student participation in discussion is low, which of the following should be done to encourage more active participation?
    a. Divide the classroom into smaller groups so that shy students will feel more comfortable speaking up.
    b. Brainstorm ideas related to the topic on the board.
    c. Allow students to lead discussion or suggest topics.
    d. All of the above

85. Ability-based differentiation involves which of the following core focus areas?
    a. How students sound out unfamiliar words
    b. How students analyze and use a reading
    c. How students self-select appropriately leveled readings
    d. How students work in peer groups

86. If diagnostic assessments indicate students have phonetic problems, which of the following activities would be best for the instructor to introduce?
    a. Activities that analyze the different aspects of words
    b. Activities that help students visualize what they read
    c. Activities that have students paraphrase and summarize texts
    d. Activities that involve using graphic organizers to identify key points and supporting details in texts

87. Which of the following is an example of interest-based differentiation?
    a. Grouping students who are all struggling with comprehending grade-level vocabulary words
    b. Grouping students who are all working on reading fluency
    c. Grouping students who are all working on sounding out unfamiliar words when reading aloud
    d. Grouping students who are all auditory learners

88. Roger has been teaching his kindergarten class new words and story structure. He uses poems and music that are focused on characters having adventures. The stories often rhyme, and the children in his class thoroughly enjoy them. What type of story is Roger using to teach his class?
    a. Myths
    b. Fairy tales
    c. Nursery rhymes
    d. Folklore

95

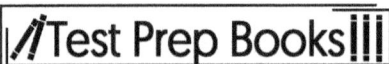

89. Mary has been reading stories aloud to her first-grade class, but she notices that some students are not as interested. She wants to have the students do some sort of activity that will be fun and encourage them to speak up. Which of the following activities would be a good way for Mary to engage her students?
    a. Use hand puppets to represent the characters in the stories while she reads.
    b. Take the students outside for a brief recess.
    c. Stop for quiet, individual reading time.
    d. Show the students a movie.

90. Teachers are asked to keep records of students' learning progress throughout the school year. Of the options below, which would be the most helpful for recording data?
    a. Notebooks
    b. Spreadsheets
    c. Report cards
    d. Word document

Constructed Response 1

Prepare an Organized Written Response to a Topic Relating to the Development of Student Literacy.

Scenario: Mr. Brown is a reading specialist at Carroll High School and assists several teachers and classes with literacy development skills. While most students seem to be writing well, Mr. Brown notices that several students in the classes seem to have trouble reading written words. These children come from a wide range of backgrounds, including native and non-native English speakers.

Task 1: What are some ways Mr. Brown can assess the students' skill levels to determine where the root of their reading issues lie?

Task 2: Describe how Mr. Brown can guide the instructors in addressing the reading issues with differentiated instruction.

Constructed Response 2

Prepare an Organized Written Response to a Case Study of an Elementary Student.

Scenario: The following case study is focused on Caleb, a second-grade student.

Caleb's primary instructor has noticed that when Caleb reads material aloud in class, he will often take long pauses and read the sentences slower than the other students. This sometimes causes him to stutter or hesitate during longer sentences. Another issue is that sometimes he will switch the order of the words he sees, for example, putting the word *the* after the word *cat* in a sentence. Despite this, Caleb is very bright and seems to fully grasp the context of the material. He also appears to be engaged when answering questions but is hesitant when having to read in front of the class.

Caleb's teacher has requested that Mr. Breiner, the reading specialist, evaluate Caleb to understand what might be causing his issues. While Caleb is highly intelligent, the teacher is wondering whether his problems with reading may indicate a reading disorder. Mr. Breiner has been requested to present ideas on how to help Caleb's reading skills improve. The teacher wants to be able to learn how to address

Practice Test

reading issues like Caleb's in the future, or at least be able to identify core literary issues very early in the developmental stage.

Use the information in the scenario and the document below to write a reply in which you use your understanding of literacy assessment and instructional strategies to examine this case study. Your response should completely address the following tasks:

Teacher notes:

- When reading the sentence, "The next-door neighbors adopted the cat that had been homeless," Caleb switched *the* and *cat*. He also seemed to take longer to sound out *homeless*.

- Longer sentences seem to cause Caleb confusion when reading aloud.

- In some of his writing responses, Caleb will sometimes switch the letters within the words or the words themselves.

- Caleb understands material clearly and gives insightful thoughts aloud. No speech problems were observed.

Task 1: Identify methods of observation that may indicate whether or not Caleb has a learning disorder. What kind of assessments can be used to determine if his reading difficulties are tied to specific written English structures or if his pausing indicates other psychological disconnects?

Task 2: Based on Caleb's reading difficulties, what are some teaching strategies that can be used to help him improve? Provide details on why differentiating Caleb's instruction would be a major step in bolstering his reading ability.

Constructed Response 3

Prepare an Organized Written Response to Instruct Teachers on What Process to Use.

Scenario: The teachers in an elementary school are proactively trying to implement content-area reading instruction in their classrooms. Their goal is to better their students' writing skills and increase comprehension and writing fluency. However, their budget is low, and the implementation must be cost-effective.

Task 1: Briefly provide an example of content-area reading instruction and describe the process in full detail while aligning the process with the budget constraints.

Task 2: Talk about how this instruction will align with an increase in comprehension and writing fluency for the entire school.

Answer Explanations

1. A: The *sh* is an example of a consonant digraph. Consonant digraphs are combinations of two or three consonants that work together to make a single sound. Examples of consonant digraphs are *sh*, *ch*, and *th*. Choice B, sound segmentation, is used to identify component phonemes in a word, such as separating the /t/, /u/, and /b/ in tub. Choice C, vowel digraph, is a set of two vowels that make up a single sound, such as *ow*, *ae*, or *ie*. Choice D, rime, is the sound that follows a word's onset, such as the /at/ in *cat*.

2. D: Sound segmentation is the identification of all the component phonemes in a word. An example would be the student identifying each separate sound, /t/, /u/, and /b/, in the word *tub*. Choice A, sound blending, is the blending together of two or more sounds in a word, such as /ch/ or /sh/. Choice B, substitution, occurs when a phoneme is substituted within a word for another phoneme, such as substituting the sound /b/ in *bun* to /r/ to create *run*. Choice C, rhyming, is an effective tool to utilize during the analytic phase of phonics development because rhyming words are often identical except for their beginning letters.

3. A: The alphabetic principle is the understanding that letters represent sounds in words. It is through the alphabetic principle that students learn the interrelationships between letter-sound (grapheme-phoneme) correspondences, phonemic awareness, and early decoding skills (such as sounding out and blending letter sounds).

4. D: Print awareness includes all of the answer choices except the spelling of sight words. Print awareness includes Choice A, the differentiation of uppercase and lowercase letters, so that students can understand which words begin a sentence. Choice B, the identification of word boundaries, is also included in print awareness; that is, students should be made aware that words are made up of letters and that spaces appear between words, etc. Choice C, the proper tracking of words, is also included in print awareness; this is the realization that print is organized in a particular way, so books must be tracked and held accordingly.

5. D: Option I, word boundaries, is one of the factors modeled because as teachers point to individual words, they indicate separation between the words. Directionality is the ability to track words as they are being read, so this is also modeled. One-to-one correspondence, the last factor listed, is the ability to match written letters to words to spoken words when reading. It is another thing teachers model when they point to words while they read.

6. B: Structural analysis focuses on the meaning of morphemes. Morphemes include base words, prefixes, and word endings (inflections and suffixes) that are found within longer words. Students can use structural analysis skill to find familiar word parts within an unfamiliar word in order to decode the word and determine the definition of the new word. The prefix im- (meaning not) in the word "improbable" can help students derive the definition of an event that is not likely to occur.

7. B: The student is performing at the phonetic stage. Phonetic spellers will spell a word as it sounds. The speller perceives and represents all of the phonemes in a word. However, because phonetic spellers have limited sight word vocabulary, irregular words are often spelled incorrectly.

Answer Explanations

8. B: The creation of word walls, Choice *I*, is advantageous during the phonetic stage of spelling development. On a word wall, words that share common consonant-vowel patterns or letter clusters are written in groups. Choices *II* and *III*, daily reading and writing opportunities, are also important in spelling instructions. Students need daily opportunities in order to review and practice spelling development. Daily journals or exit tickets are cognitive writing strategies effective in helping students reflect on what they have learned. A spelling inventory, Choice *IV*, is different than a traditional spelling test because students are not allowed to study the words prior to the administration of a spelling inventory. Therefore, this option is incorrect as it mentions the inventory contains words students have studied all week.

9. A: The teacher should have the student use a think-aloud to verbalize the directions of the shapes used when writing each letter. During think-alouds, teachers voice the metacognitive process that occurs when writing each part of a given letter. Students should be encouraged to do likewise when practicing writing the letters.

10. D: Teachers should capitalize on the transfer of relevant skills from the learner's original language(s). In this way, extra attention and instructional emphasis can be applied toward the teaching of sounds and meanings of words that are nontransferable between the two languages.

11. C: Writing samples are the most appropriate assessment of spelling for students who are performing at the pre-phonetic stages. During this stage, students participate in pre-communicative writing, which appears to be a jumble of letter-like forms rather than a series of discrete letters. Samples of students' pre-communicative writing can be used to assess their understanding of the alphabetic principle and their knowledge of letter-sound correspondences.

12. A: Phonological awareness is best assessed through identification of rimes or onsets within words. Instruction of **phonological awareness** includes detecting and identifying word boundaries, onsets/rimes, syllables, and rhyming words.

13. A: The identification of morphemes within words occurs during the instruction of structural analysis. Structural analysis is a word recognition skill that focuses on the meanings of word parts, or morphemes, during the introduction of a new word. Choice *B*, syllabic analysis, is a word analysis skill that helps students split words into syllables. Choice *C*, phonics, is the direct correspondence between and blending of letters and sounds. Choice *D*, the alphabetic principle, teaches that letters or other characters represent sounds.

14. B: Homophones are words that are pronounced the same way but differ in meaning and/or spelling. To and too are homophones because they are pronounced the same way but differ in both meaning and spelling. Choices *A*, *C*, and *D* are not homophones because they do not sound the same when spoken aloud.

15. B: Nursery rhymes are used in kindergarten to develop phoneme recognition. Rhyming words are often almost identical except for their beginning letter(s), so rhyming is a great strategy to implement during the analytic phase of phoneme development.

16. B: High-frequency words are taught during the instruction of sight word recognition. Sight words, sometimes referred to as high-frequency words, are words that are used often but may not follow the regular principles of phonics. Sight words may also be defined as words that students are able to recognize and read without having to sound out.

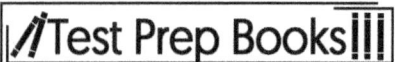

Answer Explanations

17. C: Both *A* and *B*. Decoding should be assessed in context in addition to isolation. To assess in context, students read passages from appropriate texts aloud to the teacher so that the teacher can analyze their approach to figuring out unknown words. Decoding should also be assessed in isolation. In these types of assessments, students are given a list of words and/or phonics patterns. Initially, high-frequency words that follow predictable phonics patterns are presented. The words that are presented become more challenging as a student masters less difficult words.

18. D: Sight vocabulary refers to the words a person can correctly recognize and pronounce when reading. Poor word recognition, insufficient background knowledge, or an insufficient amount of content vocabulary can all affect someone's sight vocabulary. Correct pronunciation can influence a person's skill in spelling a specific word, but the opposite is less likely, as most people can still pronounce words well even if they don't spell it correctly.

19. A: There is a positive correlation between a student's exposure to text and the academic achievement of that individual. Therefore, students should be given ample opportunities to read independently as much text as possible in order to gain vocabulary and background knowledge.

20. C: By definition, morphology is the identification and use of morphemes such as root words and affixes. Listening comprehension refers to the processes involved in understanding spoken language. Word consciousness refers to the knowledge required for students to learn and effectively utilize language. Textual analysis is an approach that researchers use to gain information and describe the characteristics of a recorded or visual message.

21. A: Phonological awareness refers to a child's ability to understand and use familiar sounds in their social environment in order to form coherent words. Phonemes are defined as distinct sound units in any given language. Phonemic substitution is part of phonological awareness—a child's ability to substitute specific phonemes for others. Blending skills refers to the ability to construct or build words from individual phonemes by blending the sounds together in a unique sequence.

22. C: When children begin to recognize and apply sound-letter relationships independently and accurately, they are demonstrating a growing mastery of phonics. Phonics is the most commonly used method for teaching people to read and write by associating sounds with their corresponding letters or groups of letters, using a language's alphabetic writing system. Syllabication refers to the ability to break down words into their individual syllables. The study of onsets and rimes strives to help students recognize and separate a word's beginning consonant or consonant-cluster sound, the onset, from the word's rime, the vowel and/or consonants that follow the onset. A grapheme is a letter or a group of letters in a language that represent a sound.

23. D: Breaking down words into their individual parts, studying prefixes, suffixes, root words, rimes, and onsets, are all examples of word analysis. When children analyze words, they develop their vocabulary and strengthen their spelling and reading fluency.

24. B: Spelling conventions is the area of study that involves mechanics, usage, and sentence formation. Mechanics refers to spelling, punctuation, and capitalization. Usage refers to the use of the various parts of speech within sentences, and sentence formation is the order in which the various words in a sentence appear. Generally speaking, word analysis is the breaking down of words into morphemes and word units in order to arrive at the word's meaning. Morphemes are the smallest units of a written language that carry meaning, and phonics refers to the study of letter-sound relationships.

Answer Explanations

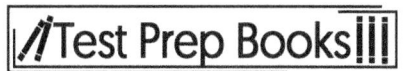

25. D: A schema is a framework or structure that stores and retrieves multiple, interrelated learning elements as a single packet of knowledge. Children who have greater exposure to life events have greater schemas. Thus, students who bring extensive background knowledge to the classroom are likely to experience easier automation when reading. In this way, background knowledge and reading comprehension are directly related. Likewise, students who have greater background knowledge are able to learn a greater number of new concepts at a faster rate.

26. A: Practice is an essential component of effective fluency instruction. A student's accuracy and rate will likely increase if a teacher provides for them opportunities to learn words and use word-analysis skills. Oral reading accompanied by guidance and feedback from teachers, peers, or parents has a significant positive impact on fluency. In order to be beneficial, such feedback needs to target specific areas in which students need improvement, as well as strategies that students can use in order to improve their areas of need. Such feedback increases students' awareness so that they can independently make needed modifications to improve fluency.

27. A: Syntax refers to the arrangement of words and phrases to form well-developed sentences and paragraphs. Semantics has to do with language meaning. Grammar is a composite of all systems and structures utilized within a language and includes syntax, word morphology, semantics, and phonology. Cohesion and coherence of oral and written language are promoted through a full understanding of syntax, semantics, and grammar.

28. B: Informal reading assessments allow teachers to create differentiated assessments that target reading skills of individual students. In this way, teachers can gain insight into a student's reading strengths and weaknesses. Informal assessments can help teachers decide what content and strategies need to be targeted. However, standardized reading assessments provide all students with the same structure to assess multiple skills at one time. Standardized reading assessments cannot be individualized. Such assessments are best used for gaining an overview of student reading abilities.

29. D: Students within a single classroom come with various background knowledge, interests, and needs. Thus, it's unrealistic to find texts that apply to all. Students benefit when a wide range of fiction and nonfiction texts are available in a variety of genres, promoting differentiated instruction.

30. D: This answer alludes to both read-alouds and think-alouds. Modeling fluency can be done through read-alouds. Proper pace, phrasing, and expression of text can be modeled when teachers read aloud to their students. During think-alouds, teachers verbalize their thought processes when orally reading a selection. The teacher's explanations may describe strategies they use as they read to monitor their comprehension. In this way, teachers explicitly model the metacognition processes that good readers use to construct meaning from a text.

31. A: Reading fluency is the ability to accurately read at a socially acceptable pace and with proper expression. Phonetic awareness leads to the proper pronunciation of words and fluency. Once students are able to read fluently, concentration is no longer dedicated toward the process of reading. Instead, students can concentrate on the meaning of a text. Thus, in the developmental process of reading, comprehension follows fluency.

32. A: Poems are an effective method for teaching fluency, since rhythmic sounds and rhyming words build a child's understanding of phonemic awareness.

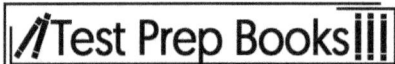

Answer Explanations

33. D: Accuracy is measured as the percentage of words that are read correctly within a given text. Word-reading accuracy is often measured by counting the number of errors that occur per 100 words of oral reading. This information is used to select the appropriate level of text for an individual.

34. B: Nonfiction texts include memoirs, biographies, autobiographies, and journalism. Choices A, C, and D are all examples of fictional prose.

35. A: Summative assessments are formal assessments that are given at the end of a unit of study. These assessments are usually longer in length. They are not completed daily. These summative assessments shouldn't be confused with informal assessments, which are used more frequently to determine mastery of the day's objective. However, summative assessments may be used to determine students' mastery in order to form intervention groups thereafter.

36. D: Boldfaced, highlighted, or italicized text notifies a student when a new vocabulary word or idea is present. Subtitles and headings can also alert a student to a change in topic or idea. These features are also important when answering questions, as a student may be able to easily find the answer with these typographic features present.

37. A: English Language Learners should master vocabulary and word usages in order to fully comprehend text. Figurative language, an author's purpose, and settings are more complex areas and are difficult for English Language Learners. These areas can be addressed once ELL students understand the meanings of words. In order to master comprehension skills, vocabulary and the English language need to be mastered first, but comprehension can still be difficult. Figurative language is culture-based, and inferences may be difficult for those with a different cultural background.

38. A: Assessments should always be frequent and ongoing for all students, but especially for those with special needs. These assessments may be informal but should be given daily after direct instruction and modeling. While summative assessments are important, they should not be the first and only assessment during a unit of study; usually summative assessments come at the end of a unit. Weekly and monthly assessments are too infrequent for remediation, intervention, or identification of struggling areas.

39. D: Although the reading corner should be a restful and enjoyable place to encourage students to read independently, it does not enhance reading comprehension directly. Choices *A*, *B*, and *C* all encourage enhancement of reading comprehension. Giving students a chance to read independently allows them to choose books they enjoy, read at their own pace, and develop a lifelong enjoyment of reading.

40. B: Purposeful teacher read-alouds allow students to listen to a story for voice emphasis and tone. This will help students when they are reading independently as well. Although students may find this time restful or a chance to catch up on old work, neither is the main purpose. Students may use this time to take notes on the reading, but students should only be listening to the story being read and not doing other work.

41. B: Pragmatics is the study of what words mean in certain situations. Choice A, morphology, involves the structure and formation of words. Choice C, syntax, refers to the order of words in a sentence. Choice D, semantics, addresses the distinct meanings of words.

Answer Explanations

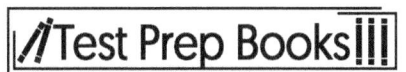

42. A: "Text evidence" refers to taking phrases and sentences directly from the text and writing them in the answer. Students are not asked to paraphrase, nor use any other resources to address the answer. Therefore, Choices *B*, *C*, and *D* are incorrect.

43. C: Phonics allows readers to effectively translate print into recognizable speech. If children lack proficiency in phonics, their ability to read fluently and to increase vocabulary will be limited.

44. D: Text-based discussions, like think-pair-share, encourage all students to speak rather than having just one student share an answer. Each student is given time to collaborate with another student and share their thoughts. It is not intended for one student to give another student the answers, which is why Choice *C* is incorrect. Although Choices *A* and *B* might be correct, they are not the MOST important reason that text-based discussions are useful in the classroom.

45. D: Extension projects and papers should be used to challenge advanced learners, not learners developing comprehension skills. Graphic organizers, taking notes, and small intervention groups can aid reading comprehension. Graphic organizers and taking notes are great ways for a student to outline key parts of the text. Small intervention groups set up by the instructor can then focus on individual needs.

46. C: Advanced students can benefit from intervention groups by allowing the students to be challenged with more complex assignments. These assignments can be worked on independently and can include more difficult questions or higher-level vocabulary. Even short projects may be beneficial for these advanced students to work on throughout the week.

47. A: Small intervention groups can benefit from a teacher reading a text or small book aloud while students listen and take notes. This helps struggling students to focus on reading comprehension rather than having to decode words. Intervention time is not meant for a teacher to give independent work nor to just provide observation without support.

48. B: Word analysis and fluency should be mastered before teaching theme, text evidence, and writing. For English Language Learners and struggling readers, word analysis and fluency are often difficult barriers, which is why comprehension skills are not initially mastered. Theme is often a complex and inferential skill, which is developed later on. Text evidence is pulling answers to comprehension questions directly from a text and cannot be accomplished until readers can fluently read and understand the text. Writing skills generally come after comprehension skills are underway.

49. D: Teachers use directed reading-thinking activities before and after reading to improve critical thinking and reading comprehension. Metacognitive skills are when learners think about their thinking. Self-monitoring is when children are asked to think as they read and ask themselves if what they have just read makes sense. KWL charts help guide students to identify what they already know about a given topic.

50. C: Asking oneself a comprehension question is a metacognition skill. Readers with metacognitive skills have learned to think about thinking. It gives students control over their learning while they read. KWL charts help students to identify what they already know about a given topic.

51. C: Listening and speaking are not part of Bloom's Taxonomy. The six parts are remembering, understanding, applying, analyzing, evaluating, and creating.

52. D: During the Emergent Spelling stage, children can identify letters but not the corresponding sounds. The other choices are all fictitious.

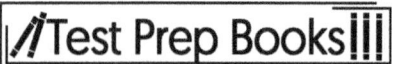

Answer Explanations

53. A: Reciprocal teaching involves predicting, summarizing, questioning, and clarifying. The other choices are all fictitious.

54. B: KWL charts are effective methods of activating prior knowledge and taking advantage of students' curiosity. Students can create a KWL (know/want to know/learned) chart to prepare for any unit of instruction and to generate questions about a topic.

55. D: Flashback is a technique used to give more background information in a story. None of the other concepts are directly related to going back in time.

56. A: Graphic organizers are methods of integrating knowledge and ideas. A graphic organizer can be one of many different visual tools for connecting concepts to help students understand information.

57. B: Making inferences is a method of deriving meaning that is intended by the author but not explicitly stated in the text. A flashback is a scene set earlier than the main story. Style is a general term for the way something is done. Figurative language is text that is not to be taken literally.

58. C: Genre is a means of categorizing text by its structure and literary elements. Fiction and nonfiction are both genre categories. Plot is the sequence of events that makes a story happen.

59. A: Scanning future portions of the text for information that helps resolve a question is an example of self-monitoring. Self-monitoring takes advantage of students' natural ability to recognize when they understand the reading and when they do not. KWL charts are used to help guide students to identify what they already know about a given topic. Metacognitive skills are when learners think about their thinking. Directed reading-thinking activities are done before and after reading to improve critical thinking and reading comprehension skills.

60. C: The five basic components of reading education are phonemic awareness, phonics, fluency, vocabulary, and comprehension.

61. B: The key word here is "inform," which is the primary purpose of all informative modes. They contain facts, definitions, instructions, and other elements with the objective purpose of informing a reader—such as study guides, instruction manuals, and textbooks. Choice A is incorrect because an argumentative mode contains language that is subjective and is intended to persuade or to inform with a persuasive bias. Choice C is incorrect as a narrative mode is used primarily to tell a story and has no intention of informing, nor is the language inherently objective. Choice D is incorrect as descriptive modes possess no inherent intent to inform, and are used primarily to describe.

62. A: Editorials, recommendation letters, and cover letters all seek to persuade a reader to agree with the author, which reflects an argumentative mode. Choice B is incorrect because the intent of the above examples is to persuade a reader to agree with the author, not to present information. Choice C is incorrect as the above examples are not trying to tell a story. Choice D is also incorrect because while the above examples may contain many descriptions, that is not their primary purpose.

63. D: Both the audience and primary purpose are important for choosing a writing mode. The audience is an important factor as the diction, tone, and stylistic choices of a written piece are tailored to fit the audience demographic. The primary purpose is the reason for writing the piece, so the mode of writing must be tailored to the most effective delivery method for the message. Choice A is incorrect because it only takes into account one of the aspects for choosing a mode and the audience, but leaves out the primary purpose. Choice B is incorrect for the same reason, except it only takes into account the primary purpose and forgets the audience. Choice C is incorrect as the main idea is the central theme or topic of the piece, which can be expressed in any form the author chooses. Because the mode depends on the reason the author wrote the piece, the main idea is not an important factor in determining which mode of writing to use.

64. C: Pathos is the rhetorical appeal that draws on an audience's emotions and sympathies. Choice A is incorrect as logos appeals to the audience's logic, reason, and rational thinking, using facts and definitions. Choice B is incorrect because ethos appeals to the audience's sense of ethics and moral obligations. Choice D is incorrect because C contains the correct answer; thus, the answer cannot be "None of the above."

65. C: The main idea of a piece is its central theme or subject and what the author wants readers to know or understand after they read. Choice A is incorrect because the primary purpose is the reason that a piece was written, and while the main idea is an important part of the primary purpose, the above elements are not developed with that intent. Choice B is incorrect because while the plot refers to the events that occur in a narrative, organization, tone, and supporting details are not used only to develop plot. Choice D is incorrect because characterization is the description of a person.

66. A: The passage describes a situation and then explains the causes that led to it. Also, it utilizes cause and effect signal words, such as *causes, factors, so,* and *as a result*. Choice B is incorrect because a compare and contrast order considers the similarities and differences of two or more things. Choice C is incorrect because spatial order describes where things are located in relation to each other. Finally, Choice D is incorrect because time order describes when things occurred chronologically.

67. B: Children and less educated audiences tend to understand short, succinct sentences more effectively because their use helps increase information processing. Choice A is incorrect as longer, more fluid sentences are best used for adults and more educated audiences because they minimize processing times and allow for more information to be conveyed. Choices C and D are incorrect because there is no correlation between a given profession and a writing style; rather, it depends on how familiar the audience is with a given subject.

68. D: Relevant information refers to information that is closely related to the subject being researched. Students might get overwhelmed by information when they first begin researching, so they should learn how to narrow down search terms for their field of study. Both Choices A and B are incorrect because they start with a range that is far too wide; the student will spend too much time sifting through unrelated information to gather only a few related facts. Choice C introduces a more limited range, but it is not closely related to the topic that is being researched. Finally, Choice D is correct because the student is choosing books that are more closely related to the topic and is using the index or table of contents to evaluate whether the source contains the necessary information.

69. A: The publisher, author, and references are elements of a resource that determine credibility. If the publisher has published more than one work, the author has written more than one piece on the subject, or the work references other recognized research, the credibility of a source will be stronger. Choice B is incorrect because the subject and title may be used to determine relevancy, not credibility, and the audience does not have much to do with the credibility of a source. Choice C is incorrect because the organization, stylistic choices, and transition words are all components of an effectively written piece, but they have less to do with credibility, other than to ensure that the author knows how to write. The length and tone of a piece are a matter of author's preference, and a work does not have to be written by multiple people to be considered a credible source.

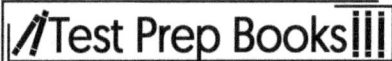

Answer Explanations

70. B: In-text citations are much shorter and usually only include the author's last name, page numbers being referenced, and for some styles, the publication year. Bibliographic citations contain much more detailed reference information. Choice A is incorrect because citations are necessary both in the text and in a bibliography. Choice C is incorrect because there are several different citation styles depending on the type of paper or article being written. Rather, students should learn when it is appropriate to apply each different style. Choice D is incorrect because all sources need to be cited regardless of medium.

71. D: The purpose of integrating research is to add support and credibility to the student's ideas, not to replace the student's own ideas altogether. Choice A is incorrect as the bulk of the paper or project should be comprised of the author's own words, and quotations and paraphrases should be used to support them. Outside sources should be included when they enhance the writer's argument, but they are not required in every single paragraph. Choice B is also incorrect because regardless of whether ideas are directly quoted or paraphrased, it is essential to always credit authors for their ideas. The use of the author's full name in every signal phrase is unnecessary, so Choice C is also incorrect.

72. D: Although there are differences between each formatting style, they all include the same basic components listed in the question for bibliography entries—the author's name, the title of the work, and its publication date. Therefore, the correct answer is all of the above.

73. C: Confidence, authenticity, and succinctness are the most important aspects of speech delivery as they instill trust in the audience and deliver a message succinctly, which reduces the likelihood that the audience's attention will wander. Choice A is incorrect as knowledge is important for a good speech, as is conviction, but appropriate vocabulary depends on the audience. The message could get lost if vocabulary is inappropriate or unfamiliar to the audience. Choice B is incorrect because though charm, wit, and connection could be useful, charming people may also be perceived as inauthentic and lose credibility with their audience. Choice D is incorrect because though compassion, empathy, and tolerance are all good qualities in a person and work well in certain speech topics, they are not inherent qualities that one must possess to deliver a good speech.

74. C: Microsoft PowerPoint is the medium that can present pictures, words, and videos because of its inherent digital format, but the vastness of the projection and presence of information can distract an audience from the presence of the speaker. Choice A is incorrect because handouts are print mediums that present information that can be taken home and reviewed later, and participants can choose to read rather than listen. Choice B is incorrect because blackboards, whiteboards, and overhead projectors allow for students to follow along with processes, but provide limited space. Choice D is incorrect because physical objects allow for participants to interact with the physical world, but they can be distracting if not properly introduced.

75. D: The age of the students is an important aspect to consider when using technology because many devices have basic requirements for motor and comprehension skills. User friendliness is important as not all students have the same amount of technological literacy. Teaching students to use a device that they will never use again is futile, so it's more practical to use technology that they will use in the real world. Choice D is the correct answer because it includes all of these aspects; Choices A, B, and C are incorrect because they only include one of the above aspects.

76. B: Collaborative learning is defined as a teaching strategy is which two or more students work together to learn something new. Choice A is incorrect because listening is not a teaching strategy so much as a learning strategy, and listening is required for most types of learning. Choice C is incorrect

Answer Explanations

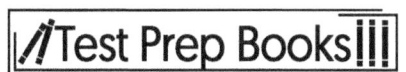

because active learning is when a student learns by doing, either by teaching another student or writing a summary. Two or more students coming together to learn actively, as opposed to one instructing the other, is more indicative of collaborative learning. Choice *D* is incorrect because although discussions may occur with two or more students, it does not usually include any form of active learning, such as creating a project or solving a problem.

77. C: One component of kinesthetic learning is students learning through physical interaction with something, such as a model or an interactive computer simulation. Choice *A* is incorrect as auditory learning is when a student learns through listening, such as listening to a lecture on a podcast. Choice *B* is incorrect because visual learning occurs when a student learns through watching or observing, such as an instructional video. Choice *D* is incorrect because distance learning occurs when the teacher and student are not in the same place and is achieved through technological means.

78. A: The revising stage involves adding, removing, and rearranging sections of a written work. Choice *B* is incorrect as the publishing stage involves the distribution of the finished product to the publisher, teacher, or reader. Choice *C* is incorrect because the writing stage is the actual act of writing the work, and generally does not including editing or revision. Choice *D* is incorrect as the pre-writing stage involves the planning, drafting, and researching of the intended piece.

79. A: The writing workshop is the teaching strategy involving a short lesson on how to write or to give the topic, an individual writing session, and then a sharing section in which the students read what they have written and listens to others. Choice *B* is incorrect because teacher modeling means being an example from which the students can imitate their writing and behavior. It requires that teachers be skilled writers themselves. Choice *C* is incorrect because the writer's notebook is the physical or digital notebook where students write and store their work. And Choice *D* is incorrect because freewriting refers to giving students a set length of time to write on a subject without editing their ideas or expressions.

80. C: Giving the students many opportunities to write is the most effective way they learn to write, and the most effective learning occurs through doing. Choice *A* is incorrect because instruction should not be standardized; it should be individualized to fit different students' needs. Choice *B* is incorrect because feedback should be specific, not generalized, so that a student may focus on the parts of their writing that need work, while also recognizing what he or she is doing well in other areas. Choice *D* is incorrect because though it can be helpful for students to evaluate and discuss each other's work, it is important to avoid creating a culture of comparison and competition in the classroom, which can lead to lower morale and negatively affect relationships between students.

81. D: Writing assessments should be conducted and returned in a timely manner so that students can learn from their mistakes, which in turn helps them to avoid repeating the same errors and developing ineffective writing habits. Choice *A* is incorrect because though it is important to present criticism in a constructive and encouraging way, it is better to integrate positive feedback with suggestions for improvement. Choice *B* is incorrect because peer review can be an effective learning tool, but only when it is properly modeled and monitored by the instructor. Choice *C* is incorrect because, although a holistic approach is one way to approach writing assessments, it is not the only useful method; in some cases, students need to focus on one specific area of improvement.

82. B: An analytic rubric is an evaluation tool that explicitly states the expectations of an assignment and breaks it down into components. Choice *A* is incorrect because a conference is a discussion, not a tool. Choice *C* is incorrect because although verbal feedback may accompany a completed rubric, it is not the

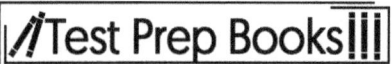

tool itself. Choice *D* is incorrect because a discussion with peers is not a tool, though it may incorporate evaluation.

83. B: Keeping discussions productive means that the instructor guides the flow of discussion to ensure adherence to the topic, which would entail preventing tangents and not engaging with the student should they wish to argue. Choice *A* is incorrect because cultivating an environment of inclusion and mutual respect involves letting everyone have a chance to speak, monitoring student behavior for respect and tolerance, and educating students on cultural differences. Choice *C* is incorrect because encouraging participation involves galvanizing the students by calling on them, writing their responses on the board, or having them create their own topic. Choice *D* is incorrect because ensuring accountability requires that students prepare for class participation by doing homework or taking quizzes, etc. and are held accountable by being assigned or deducted points.

84. D: Dividing students into smaller groups allows for shy students who are intimidated by a large group of people to feel more comfortable in participating. Allowing students to lead discussion or suggest topics gives them more responsibility while also encouraging them to prepare more for class and letting them choose topics that they are interested in. Brainstorming ideas together can give students a starting point when they do not feel confident or knowledgeable about speaking up on a topic. Therefore, *D*—all of the above—is the best answer.

85. D: Ability-based differentiation addresses three core areas of focus that determine reading proficiency and build reading skills. These include examining students' conceptual understanding of reading, how students analyze and use the reading, and how students evaluate and respond to reading. The other choices describe important skills that students develop, but they are not hallmarks of ability-based differentiation.

86. A: When students have phonetic problems, instructors should introduce activities that help the students sound out words and analyze their different aspects to build familiarity with English vocabulary and structure. The other choices would be more appropriate activities to aid reading comprehension.

87. D: Interest-based differentiation is based on the concept that students' performance can be associated with their interest level in the subject or activity. Choices *A*, *B*, and *C* are based on performance or skill level, while Choice *D* is an example of interest-based differentiation. Instructors can encourage reading growth by allowing students to choose their learning activities. Students more interested in auditory activities may find listening to oral reading exercises more engaging than reading alone in their own head.

88. C: Nursery rhymes are poems or songs that teach children new terms and stories. Choice *A* is incorrect; myths are stories told to attempt to explain the origin of something. Choice *B* is incorrect because while fairy tales can be as entertaining as nursery rhymes, they are not sung; they are short stories that sometimes contain supernatural elements. Choice *D* is incorrect because folklore are orated stories about common people.

89. A: The best way for Mary to keep her students engaged would be to use hand puppets as a supplement; this activity may spark greater engagement from both visual and kinesthetic learners. Stopping for a recess may be a good idea for a break, but it will not encourage students to engage when they get back. Stopping for individual reading time will not encourage the students to speak up and may further isolate them from engaging. Showing the students a movie might be fun, but it is more of a passive activity and will not engage students in the way Mary wants.

Answer Explanations

90. B: It is recommended that teachers keep spreadsheets to track students' progress in grades and skill development. While the other tools could be used for keeping track of data, they are not the best options. Notebooks and Word documents do not organize information as efficiently as spreadsheets, and report cards are primarily tools for students and parents (not teachers) to stay informed about the students' progress.

Index

A Five-Finger Retell Activity, 47
Ability-Based, 61, 108
Ability-Based Differentiation, 62, 95, 108
Accuracy, 39, 42, 102
Active Learning, 64, 106
Adherence to Conventions of English, 59
Advanced Literacy Stage, 15
Affix, 20, 28
Alliteration, 13, 55
Analytic, 69, 95, 98, 99, 107
Anchor Charts, 72
Annotation, 55, 73
Antagonist, 54
Appositives, 35
Auditory Learning, 64
Author's Purpose, 56, 57
Autobiography, 53, 58, 75
Background Knowledge, 35, 37, 44, 45, 46, 47, 85, 86, 100, 101
Base Words, 28
Biographies and Autobiographies, 53
Biography, 17, 53
Blending, 13, 85, 100
Cause and Effect, 58
Cause/Effect, 58
Central Or Major Characters, 54
Characters, 54
Chronological/Sequence Order, 58
Clarify, 49
Clear Organization, 59
Collaborative Learning, 64, 107
Comedy, 53
Communication, 62, 74
Comparison/Contrast, 58
Conflict, 54
Connotation, 71
Consonant Blend, 25, 27, 77
Consonant Digraphs, 26, 98
Content, 1, 2, 6, 8, 17, 26, 30, 38, 39, 48, 49, 53, 59, 60, 64, 67, 68, 71, 73, 77, 79, 85, 88, 97, 101
Content-Specific, 26, 38, 39, 77
Contextual Strategies, 35, 38, 39, 87
Conventional Stage, 22, 25, 77
Creative Writing, 54

Decoded, 29, 39
Decoding, 8, 21, 28, 31, 75, 82, 100
Denotation, 72
Description, 58
Diction, 71, 79, 104
Diction/Tone, 59
Differentiated Instruction, 61, 68
Digital Literacy, 62, 63, 64
Digital Tools, 73
Directionality, 16
Discussion, 45, 55, 63, 64, 66, 67, 72, 95, 107, 108
Distance Learning, 64, 107
Drama, 52
Dynamic Characters, 54
Early Intermediate Literacy Stage, 15
Editing Step, 72
Encoding, 21, 31, 75, 82
Explicitly, 21, 29, 40, 46, 69, 76, 95, 101, 104, 107
Expository, 56, 75
Expository Texts, 56
Feedback, 60, 68, 69, 70, 94
Figurative Language, 54, 55, 88, 90, 91, 102, 104
First-Person Point of View, 53
Flash Cards, 30, 34
Flat Character, 54
Fluency, 8, 31, 32, 33, 39, 41, 45, 66, 67, 82, 87, 89
Formative Assessment, 60, 68
Fry Graph, 34
Fry's Formula, 34, 35
Genre, 52, 86, 88, 104
Good Writing, 79
Graphemes, 40, 86
Graphic Organizers, 47, 51, 89, 103, 104
High-Frequency Words, 39, 99, 100
Holistic, 69, 94, 107
Homophones, 25, 99
How-to, 58
Inferential Comprehension, 56
Informational Text, 8, 44, 53, 57, 58
Informational Writing, 75
Interest-Based, 61, 95, 108
Intermediate Literacy Stage, 15

Index

Irregular Words, 24, 25, 28, 29, 30, 39, 77, 98
Kinesthetic Learning, 64, 107
KWL Charts, 43, 47, 51, 89, 90, 91, 103, 104
Language Comprehension, 44
Letter Recognition, 18
Level of Meaning, 35
Lexile Text Measures, 34
Listening Comprehension, 44, 85, 100
Literal Comprehension, 56
Literary Elements, 53, 91, 104
Literary Nonfiction, 53
Main Idea, 59, 92
Making Predictions, 48, 49
Manipulation of Syllables, 13
Metacognitive Strategies, 47
Morphemes, 28, 86, 98, 100
Morphological Maps, 36
Multisensory Approach, 30
Narrative Writing, 75
Narrator, 53, 54
Non-Decodable, 29, 30, 31, 32
Nonfiction Narratives, 56
Non-Print Sources, 45
One-to-One Correspondence, 16, 83, 98
Onset, 14
Order of Importance, 58
Organize, 49, 51, 109
Originality, 79
Orthography, 28
Parenthetical Elements, 35
Persuasive Text, 53
Persuasive Texts, 56
Persuasive Writing, 75
Phoneme, 14, 15, 19, 20, 21, 40, 76, 98, 99
Phoneme Deletion, 14
Phoneme Substitution, 15, 85
Phoneme-Grapheme Correspondence, 21
Phonemic Awareness, 7, 14, 24, 40, 41, 76, 98, 101, 104
Phonetic Stage, 22, 23, 24, 31, 32, 42, 43, 76, 98, 99
Phonics Instruction, 22, 39
Phonological Awareness, 13, 84, 85, 99, 100
Picture Walk, 46
Plot, 6, 46, 47, 54, 56, 75, 105
Poetic Structure, 52
Poetry, 52, 53

Point of View, 1, 53, 55, 90
Precommunicative Writing, 22, 76
Predictable Structures, 35
Prefixes, 28, 85, 98, 100
Pre-Phonetic Stage, 22, 23, 32, 84, 99
Pre-Reading Strategies, 48
Print, 16, 17, 83, 85, 98
Print Awareness, 16, 83, 85, 98
Problem/Solution, 58
Prose, 52
Prosody, 39
Protagonist, 54
Qualitative Measures, 35
Quantitative Measures, 34
Questioning, 49
Rainbow Writing, 30
Readability Formulas, 34
Reading Comprehension, 44, 46, 86
Reading Fluency, 21, 29, 39, 40, 41, 42, 43, 45, 57, 87, 95, 100
Reading Rate, 39, 86
Receptive Language Development, 15
Reciprocal Phonological Skills, 21, 32
Recursively, 21
Reference Materials, 35
Reflective Reading, 50
Return Sweeping, 16
Revision Step, 72
Rime, 14, 83
Root Word, 28, 100
Rubric, 61, 69, 95, 107
Scan, 3, 48
Schwa, 27
Second Person Point of View, 53
Segmenting, 13, 76
Semantic Organizers, 15, 51
Semiphonetic Stage, 22, 23
Sequence, 58
Setting, 20, 40, 45, 46, 47, 54, 56, 75, 95
Sight Words, 28, 29, 30, 31, 32, 40, 83, 87, 98
Skim, 35, 48, 58
Spatial Order, 58, 92
Speaker, 53, 54, 93, 106
Spelling Development, 22, 76
Storyboards, 47
Structural Analysis, 28, 36, 83, 84, 85, 86, 98, 99
Suffixes, 28, 85, 98, 100

Index

Summarize, 41, 44, 45, 46, 47, 50, 73, 95
Summative Assessment, 68, 87, 102
Supporting Details/Evidence, 59
Syllabic Analysis, 28, 84
Syllabication, 28, 84, 86
Syllables, 13, 28
Systematically, 21, 76
Teacher-Led Practice, 76
Text Evidence, 65, 89, 103
Text-Dependent Questions, 55
Thesis Statement, 57, 75
Third Person Limited, 54
Third Person Omniscient, 54
Third Person Point of View, 53
Timed-Reading, 40
Timed-Repeated Readings, 41
Tone, 39, 54, 71, 88, 92, 102, 104, 105
Tragedy, 53
Transitional Stage, 22, 24, 25
Transitional Terms, 58
Trick Words, 29
Venn Diagrams, 47, 51
Visual Aids, 51
Visual Learning, 64
Vocabulary, 8, 31, 32, 33, 35, 38, 41, 82, 85, 86, 88
Voice, 69, 71, 89, 99, 102
Word Analysis, 28, 86, 89, 103
Word Families, 27
Word Maps, 36
Word Recognition, 28, 39, 40
Word Walls, 24, 43, 76, 84
Word Webs, 15, 37, 51
Words, 4, 16, 28, 29, 38, 55
Worksheets, 30
Writer's Focus, 79
Written Expression, 79

Dear Praxis Test Taker,

Thank you again for purchasing this study guide for your Praxis Teaching Reading 5205 exam. We hope that we exceeded your expectations.

Our goal in creating this study guide was to cover all of the topics that you will see on the test. We also strove to make our practice questions as similar as possible to what you will encounter on test day. With that being said, if you found something that you feel was not up to your standards, please send us an email and let us know.

We would also like to let you know about other books in our catalog that may interest you.

Praxis Core

This can be found on Amazon: amazon.com/dp/1637759819/

Praxis Elementary Education Multiple Subjects

This can be found on Amazon: amazon.com/dp/1637750544/

We have study guides in a wide variety of fields. If the one you are looking for isn't listed above, then try searching for it on Amazon or send us an email.

Thanks Again and Happy Testing!
Product Development Team
info@studyguideteam.com

FREE Test Taking Tips Video/DVD Offer

To better serve you, we created videos covering test taking tips that we want to give you for FREE. **These videos cover world-class tips that will help you succeed on your test.**

We just ask that you send us feedback about this product. Please let us know what you thought about it—whether good, bad, or indifferent.

To get your **FREE videos**, you can use the QR code below or email freevideos@studyguideteam.com with "Free Videos" in the subject line and the following information in the body of the email:

    a. The title of your product

    b. Your product rating on a scale of 1-5, with 5 being the highest

    c. Your feedback about the product

If you have any questions or concerns, please don't hesitate to contact us at info@studyguideteam.com.

Thank you!

www.ingramcontent.com/pod-product-compliance
Lightning Source LLC
Chambersburg PA
CBHW081203240426
43669CB00039B/2799